AGAINST ALL AUTHORITY
Anarchism and the Literary Imagination

Jeff Shantz

imprint-academic.com

Published in the UK by Imprint Academic
PO Box 200, Exeter EX5 5YX, UK

Published in the USA by Imprint Academic
Philosophy Documentation Center
PO Box 7147, Charlottesville, VA 22906-7147, USA

ISBN 978 184540 237 2

A CIP catalogue record for this book is available from the
British Library and US Library of Congress

For Michael Dunwoody

Contents

Acknowledgements

This was truly a labor of love. It gave me the opportunity to engage with a range of writers, theorists, and organizers who have influenced me greatly over the years. It also allowed me to read anew some often overlooked classics. This was a work that I literally carried with me over time and space. Various parts of the book were written in Nanaimo, Hope, Harrison Hot Springs, Chilliwack, and Merritt, as well as my home city Surrey, British Columbia.

I must offer a special thanks to my wonderful children Saoirse and Molly Shantz who are always supportive and understanding. They create an incredibly creative and vibrant environment in which to live, work, and play. This book is dedicated to Michael Dunwoody, one of the first to spur and encourage the literary imagination in a working class kid.

Against all authority

Anarchism and the literary imagination

The specter of anarchism has long haunted the troubled dreams of political authorities and economic elites. Anarchy, the philosophy that non-elites can effectively govern their own affairs in the absence of instituted leaders, has spooked state rulers of the capitalist and so-called socialist nations alike, who have devoted considerable resources to extinguish it. The belief that anarchism had been vanquished in the mid twentieth century proved to be mistaken. In the last decades of the twentieth century and the first decades of the twenty-first, the ghost of anarchy has recently enjoyed a stunning resurgence. Anarchism has provided much of the political inspiration for the alternative globalization movements that have emerged since the 1990s, particularly within the movements that have arisen in the liberal democracies of the global North. Alternative globalization activists, seeking alternatives to the failed projects of statist socialism and communism, have found in anarchism a political perspective that challenges capitalism, liberal democracy, and the traditional leftist movements alike.

At the same time the return of anarchism has also spurred an often violent backlash from instituted political and economic authorities who are fully aware of the potency of the anarchist challenge to states, capital, and the elite ideologies that justify their rule. The discourses of government spokespeople, police officers, corporate media, and business public relations documents have presented anarchists as nothing less than a threat to civilization itself. Mainstream media has depicted anarchists, particularly street protesters during meetings of global capital such as the World Trade Organization and International Monetary Fund, as hooligans, degenerates, rioters, and gangsters. These fevered depictions recall the language of the first "red scares" and suggest that anarchists once again stand at the center of paranoiac fears within state capitalist moral panics.

Unfortunately the uniform chorus of condemnation of anarchy from various elites has served to obscure the actual perspectives and practices of a major social movement. It has also served to dismiss the interests and motives of thousands of political actors from a range of social and geographical backgrounds. While anarchism is presented by opponents as a destructive movement based on anger, proponents know it as a richly creative movement based on mutual aid and affinity. Even more, the diversity of anarchist interests and its holistic approach to social change is overlooked. Far from being a straightforward political movement, concerned with political issues narrowly conceived, anarchism has contributed to movements in literature, art, and culture more broadly. Yet anarchist engagements with creative movements and cultural production have largely been overlooked. Attention to anarchist contributions to creative work provides needed insight into anarchist movements and their perspectives on and contributions to broader social change. It also poses important challenges to dominant cultural traditions within state capitalist societies and offers a glimpse into a promising alternative for radically transformed social relationships against the hierarchical, unequal, and unjust structures that have long characterized statist and capitalist societies.

Against All Authority provides an opportunity to rethink anarchist ideas and initiatives. It offers something of a corrective to the limited portrayals of anarchy that have dominated for far too long. The book examines historical and contemporary engagements of anarchism and literary production. Anarchists have used literary production to express opposition to values and relations characterizing advanced capitalist (and socialist) societies while also expressing key aspects of the alternative values and institutions proposed within anarchism. Among favored themes are anarchist critiques of corporatization, inequality, and patriarchal relations as well as explorations of developing anarchist perspectives on revolution, ecology, sexuality, and mutual aid. These are inspired by and serve to inspire the anarchist imagination.

A central feature of anarchist perspectives is the belief that means and ends should correspond. Thus, in anarchist literature as in anarchist politics, a radical approach to form is as important as content. Anarchist literature joins other critical approaches to creative production in attempting to break down divisions between readers and writer, audience and artist, encouraging all to become active participants in shared creative processes. Engaging with creative anarchist endeavors, in which literary production is part of a holistic approach to everyday resistance, provides insights into the dreams, desires and concerns of those who pursue positive social change. It also allows a greater understanding of alternative worldviews in the contemporary period. In anarchist movements the literary imagination plays a rich part, as glimpse into ongoing anarchist histories show.

Against hegemony: toward anarchy

The need for imaginative criticism is ever more pressing. Issues like industrial poisoning and nuclear threats take precedence, for many working people, over more immediate concerns for subsistence, such as poverty and the exploitation of labor, even of their own labor. For anarchist social critic, Paul Goodman (1994, 3): "This is significant because the great revolutionary motivation of physical pain and immediate distress in America, diminished; the biological dangers that are cried up require imagination to understand." At the same time the forces of distress can create a sense of despair, defeatism or futility discouraging social change.

The ideological surround of state capitalism can be overwhelming, presenting a sense of capitalism as a natural, unchangeable system. The ideology of state capital as the only world, let alone the best of all possible worlds, reinforced in media, legal, educational, political, and economic discourses is hegemonic — it dominates views and understandings of the world and its structures (political, economic, environmental, social, and cultural). The power of this hegemony of state capitalism is such that it can become difficult for people to even imagine alternatives, let alone have the confidence to attempt to pursue the alternatives that they might envision or hope for.

At the present time there is, at least in the global North, no revolutionary spirit, no expression of radical counter-movements capable of broad social transformation (rather than protest movements). There is no organized counter-force that might realistically challenge states and capital, few of what I term "infrastructures of resistance" that might sustain struggles against states and capital over time and place (Shantz 2010a). Even less can there be said to be a "revolutionary culture" or even "radical culture" that infuses society as in previous periods of broad social upheaval and transformation.

For large numbers of people, detached from community, or even neighborhood, alienated and exploited, talk of change is more than hopeless, it is unsettling. Paul Goodman (1994, 5) suggests that where there is no realistic alternative, even the suggestion of social change can rouse anxiety. Anxiety further hampers imagination and initiative.

Moments of crisis evoke panicked responses but things quickly return to business as usual. Few are moved to change their conditions of life. The movements that spring up around moments of state capitalist spectacle, that become part of the spectacle, do not resonate more broadly with diverse cross-sections of the population. They do not stir the imagination or move the spirit. Neither do they provide lasting means of expression to incite, engage, or encourage the population(s) that they would seek, or claim to seek, to inspire.

Media and arts and letters become part of the bureaucratic administration of things (an irony in view of Engels who saw that as communism): standard commodities for private consumption. Created for profit, arts and letters become means for profit—either as objects themselves, or as commodities to aid in the circulation of capital (advertizing). Concerns for profit and administration dominate taste, style, communication and education—the circulation of ideas most broadly. Practices and forms of discourse and intercourse that were previously rooted in community life, material needs, or spontaneous expressions of personal creativity have become products of multinational, billion dollar corporate conglomerates with something to sell.

Meaningful interpretations of human experience are eclipsed by considerations of markets, exchange and surplus value. In terms of the market, for Goodman:

> Its moral justification is really a self-proving superstition; it 'solves' in its own style problems that it has created itself; its research is incestuously staffed from its own bureaucrats who work for their own aggrandizement and cannot see anything else. (Goodman 1994, 6)

These have become the new myths, the new religions.

Where there is no sense of real alternatives, of realistic possibilities for different ways of doing things in a way that sustains people in the longer term, anarchists have long noted, partly due to the conviction that under current circumstances, and given the current balance of forces, that a radical attempt at broad social change would end badly. As Goodman (ibid., 5) suggests: "Any revolutionary action, it is deeply believed, must use the same methods and must come out with the same results as being part of a very similar machine." Here the incapacity of radical visions to rise beyond the failed experiments and disastrous models of previous, typically authoritarian, practice, weighs heavily on present, and future, expressions of revolutionary desire.

For Goodman, this is related to the radical imaginary:

> Partly, it is that there is a lack of social imagination *of* alternatives to the way of life. As I have frequently argued, this lack of imagination, the sentiment that 'Nothing Can Be Done,' is self-causing and self-proving in the very conditions that the critics attack. (ibid., 4)

Social change requires a certain inspiration as much as an analysis of conditions.

Cracking state capitalist hegemony requires more than appeals to reason or the presentation of detailed analysis and evidence. Many people, perhaps most, already know that capitalism is a profoundly unjust social arrangement. For many anarchists, pure politics is never enough. Politics must inspire the passions. It must draw upon the imagination as well as the intellect. In the words of DIY anarchist Professor Calamity:

> I don't trust political people who don't appreciate fiction. Too much of our politics, even anarchist politics, lacks imagination. The problems are so numbing in their complexity and scope that we *need* to be able to draw upon the most imaginative solutions possible to have any chance. I also believe that fiction tends to be more effective propaganda for the extreme left than Noam Chomskyesque critiques. (Quoted in Killjoy 2009, 74)

Fiction will always inspire practical politics in important ways. For Professor Calamity:

> Fiction can speak to the heart, something that's much needed for anarchist struggles. We're talking about a radical change, not just in economic terms but also in how we relate to each other and the world. I would think fiction would be better at articulating this than non-fiction. It is not surprising to me that totalitarian regimes like the Nazis, Italian Fascists, Bolsheviks, etc. first ban (and then burn) fiction works as dangerous. Fiction has a strange power to move people and 'stick' with them. (ibid., 75)

For the great anarchist agitator and organizer, Emma Goldman, literature, poetry, and drama provide ways to reach new, otherwise inaccessible, audiences. They also provide engaging and exciting ways to speak with people beyond polemic and diatribe. Over time, Goldman lost faith in what she called "the wonder worker" — the spoken word, political speech, the soapbox — that had contributed so much to her own popularity and notoriety. Instead Goldman moved to emphasize the power of print, the mobilizing capacity of literature. Literature is a key part of the 'terrible struggle of the thinking man and woman against political, social and moral conventions' (Goldman 1972, 111). In Goldman's view:

> The very fact that most people attend meetings only if aroused by newspaper sensations, or because they expect to be amused, is proof that they really have no inner urge to learn. It is altogether different with the written mode of human expression. (ibid., 14)

For Goldman, literature matches the creative, inspiring, elevating basis of love. This provides the force for a new world itself (ibid., 167).

The question, for anarchists, is not how to achieve, maintain and administer power, as many leftists claim, but, rather, to awaken and inspire initiative — the real fount of power. As Goodman stresses:

> Despite the prevalent superstition to the contrary, there could be alternative ways of modern life, and some of the critics propose them, but the point is for people to feel themselves differently than they do. (Goodman 1994, 7)

Anarchists seek to ignite the fires of initiative. Anarchists, stressing the free, direct, voluntary participation of people in the matters of decision that impact their lives — that people have the capacity to make themselves and their communities — always depend on the creativity, inventiveness and courage of human initiative. This is the force of, for example, do-it-yourself (DIY) in anarcho-punk literature, art and music. It also speaks to the ongoing connections between anarchism and literary production. For anarchists, the literary imagination has played a key part in this.

The truly anarchist literature means what it says and expects that it will make a difference (ibid., 60). Anarchist genres often seek, or succeed, to make something of community. There is a strong sense expressed in anarchist criticism that not only is this or that specific issue a problem, but, rather, the overall arrangement of social life. Anarchist criticism includes various forms — revolutionary, utopian, apocalyptic. The apocalyptic literature of primitivism, the poetic terrorism of postmodern anarchy — they offer, at least, an emotional call for insurrection.

Anarchism provides a vital alternative — a way of understanding the world that challenges the assertions of state capitalist hegemony while suggesting that things can be (and have been) done differently and better. At its best it provides realistic visions for a different world that might be realized in fact. Anarchists undermine aspects of state capitalist hegemony, acting, and writing in a corrosive manner against capitalist ideology. Anarchism encourages openness to new experiences and perspectives, experimentation with style and form.

Anarchy is order

One of the difficulties in properly understanding anarchism has been that both popular and academic portrayals of anarchism typically, rather badly, misrepresent anarchist movements and ideas. The most familiar image of anarchism is perhaps the black trench coat-wearing man of shadows holding a bomb. This symbol is presented in works of fiction such as *The Secret Agent* and *The Man Who Was Thursday* as well as in popular media accounts. It is one that has returned in the twenty-first century as anarchism has enjoyed a revival in the context of alternative globalization politics. Not merely a manifestation of public fear or moral panic, the anarchist as man-with-a-bomb has recently made a comeback in academic literature on terrorism since 9/11 (Gelvin 2008, 2010).

The image of the anarchist bomb thrower is closely associated with another, more academic, misrepresentation of anarchist thought. That is, as Lyman Tower Sargent (1983) notes, the misconception that anarchism is merely individualism or nihilism, the philosophy of the detached individual. In fact, most of anarchist thought has emphasized cooperation and communal or collective action against the detached individualism promoted by capitalist rhetoric.

For anarchists, society is not a simple grouping of individuals. Neither does anarchy suggest society will be unorganized. On the contrary, anarchists stress that most of social life, even in archic societies, is built on voluntary relations of support and care in which neighbors look out for neighbors and people interact on the basis of mutually peaceful recognition. The most significant and influential theoretical works of anarchism, *Mutual Aid, State and Anarchy,* and *Anarchism in Action,* are all detailed analyses of the central place of cooperation in human societies and the significance of mutual aid and support in human development, individual and social.

In order to understand anarchism and the literary imagination it is necessary to outline some of the key themes and approaches in anarchist thought more broadly. One might begin with a rather poetic offering from the anarchist author John Henry MacKay who describes anarchy as follows:

ANARCHY
Ever reviled, accursed, ne'er understood,
Thou art the grisly terror of our age.
'Wreck of all order,' cry the multitude,
'Art thou, and war and murder's endless rage.'
O, let them cry. To them that ne'er have striven
The truth that lies behind a word to find,
To them the word's right meaning was not given.
They shall continue blind among the blind.
But thou, O word, so clear, so strong, so pure,
Thou sayest all which I for goal have taken.
I give thee to the future! Thine secure
When each at least unto himself shall waken.
Come it in sunshine? In the tempest's thrill?
I cannot tell—but it the earth shall see!
I am an Anarchist! Wherefore I will
Not rule, and also ruled I will not be! (Quoted in Goldman 1972, 47)

The word "anarchy" comes from the ancient Greek term "anarchos" and means "without a ruler." While ruling elites, not surprisingly, proclaim that the end of rule will inevitably lead to a descent into chaos and turmoil, anarchists maintain that external, authoritarian rule is unnecessary for the preservation of order. Rather than a descent into a Hobbesian war of all against all, a society without instituted government authority suggests to anarchists the very possibility for creative and peaceful human relations. Pierre-Joseph Proudhon, the first to identify positively his theory as anarchist, neatly summarized the anarchist perspective in his famous slogan: "Anarchy is Order."

Peter Kropotkin, the most significant anarchist theorist, offered the following influential definition of anarchism as:

> the name given to a principle or theory of life and conduct under which society is conceived without government—harmony in such a society being obtained, not by submission to law, or by obedience to any authority, but by free agreements concluded between the various groups, territorial and professional, freely constituted for the sake of production and consumption, as also for the satisfaction of the infinite variety of needs and aspirations of a civilized being. (Kropotkin 1910, 914)

Another definition is provided by individualist anarchist James J. Martin, who notes certain commonalities in anarchism, despite the overall diversity of anarchist thought. For Martin:

> When anarchism in its several forms, including its theoretical statements and practical experiments, is analyzed structurally, it generally

separates into three broad areas of tactics and strategy: (a) a rejection of constituted authority as the source of social dynamism and equilibrium; (b) a refusal to collaborate with the existing order anywhere through participation in any program of reformism; (c) the promotion of a variety of noncoercive alternatives of quite clearly defined nature as a substitute. (Martin 1970, vii)

Anarchists base their analysis of social relations on the importance of voluntary rather than coercive interaction. For anarchists, coercion cannot provide the basis for freedom. Coercive interaction has only negative results over time. Coercion negatively impacts humans at the emotional and the behavioral levels. Real freedom can only be realized through voluntary relations and interactions. According to Lyman Tower Sargent: "Anarchism is a political philosophy contending that no one (individual or group) should hold coercive authority" (1983, 6). For anarchists, social problems result from the fact that people are not allowed to direct their own lives according to the needs of themselves and their communities. Too much time and energy are expended and lost in trying to control others (for authorities) and in trying to escape control by others (for subordinates). This is not merely an effect of political or economic power. It extends to other spheres of life, including personal relationships, the family, schools, and culture more broadly.

For anarchists, the regulatory and supervisory mechanisms of the state are especially suited to producing docile and dependent subjects. Through institutions like courts and prisons, but also social policies and ideological media, authorities extend the practices of ruling from control over bodies to influence over minds. Moral regulation provides a subtle means for nurturing repression and conformity. It can contribute to the development of relations of dependence rather than self-determination, as practices of the state increasingly come to be viewed as the only legitimate mechanisms for solving disputes or addressing social needs. For anarchists the "rule of law" administered through the institutions of the state is not the guarantor of freedom, but, rather, freedom's enemy, closing off alternative avenues for human interaction, creativity, and community while containing more and more people within its own bounds.

Anarchism is more than a rejection of authority, however. It also founds its politics on the recognition of the positive benefits of voluntary cooperation and mutual aid. Not a reactive position (against authority), anarchism is a positive theory (*for* mutuality and solidarity). In the absence of direct authority and power (state or police) people tend to get along, going about their affairs without interfering with or bothering others. Under such circumstances, broadly extended, society can thrive.

In times of crisis, social or natural, when it might be expected that people would be at their most self-serving and opportunistic, it turns out that people tend to come together, in the absence of the state, to look after one another and help one another out. Examples such as Hurricane Katrina and the British Petroleum oil spill in the Gulf of Mexico show this, as do numerous other examples.

As the anarchist theorist Colin Ward suggests:

> Given a common need, a collection of people will, by trial and error, by improvisation and experiment, evolve order out of chaos— this order being more durable than any kind of externally imposed order. (Ward 1966, 103)

People tend to stand by and take responsibility for decisions that they have been actively involved in arriving at. Even more, they tend to view these decisions as being more legitimate and far more reasonable than decisions that are imposed from outside. This sort of order cannot be coercive. Instead it is: "(1) voluntary, (2) functional, (3) temporary, and (4) small" (ibid., 101). This provides the basis for a radical, even revolutionary politics that is distinct from the statist, party-based politics of the authoritarian variants of socialism and communism.

Anarchism has developed an approach unique in revolutionary or leftist politics. While these politics have tended to emphasize the industrial or so-called productive spheres of life, anarchism has long focused on so-called domestic or non-industrial spheres. Mutual aid and care have always been at the center of anarchist theory and politics. Anarchists have taken radical analysis beyond the typical realms of politics (state) and economy (market) that have dominated radical movements on the left more broadly. Thus, very early on, anarchists have given serious attention to the family, sex, education, and relationships, as sites of strength and struggle.

Anarchism is marked by two primary overall tendencies. The first, and predominant, is collective or social anarchism. The second, a minority today, and within the history of anarchism, is philosophical or individualist anarchism with its emphasis on individual liberty and personal transformation. Social anarchism focuses on equality and social transformation through collective effort, including the possibility of revolutionary action. Philosophical anarchism places greater emphasis on individual freedom to act unfettered by the constraints of social mores and norms. Philosophical anarchism also differs from social anarchism in its distrust of social organization, including the mass organizing for radical or revolutionary social change preferred by socialists and social anarchists. It is philosophical anarchism, with its emphasis on personal innovation and creativity that has inspired artists such as Eugene O'Neill, and James Joyce, though Joyce also engages with revolutionary syndicalism. Others, such as Ursula K. LeGuin, have been inspired by social anarchism and the theories of Peter Kropotkin.

There emerge productive tensions in the understandings of how anarchism might address the real world and/or the world of fiction. Is anarchy a call to literary and intellectual freedom or a vision of political organizing? Differences emerge over views of the role of art and literature and the responsibility of the artist (and/or activist). For many anarchists, writing is part of their political work. Many take an individual approach, producing and distributing their work in do-it-yourself networks outside mainstream publishing channels and commercial markets. Anarchist author Ursula K. LeGuin offers a brief description of the anarchist: "One who, choosing, accepts the responsibility of choice" (quoted in Killjoy 2009, 12). The most striking and memorable fiction has always been ungovernable, representing a sense of risk. And this too well describes anarchy.

Anarchism and the literary imagination

Anarchists have spoken to both literary creation and the connections between literature, literary production, and society and social change. Anarchist writings on literature, and indeed anarchist literature, have received much less attention and been the subject of much less discussion than has Marxist literary criticism, which has, indeed, become an established part of the academic canon in literary criticism. Similarly the anarchist aspects of literature (and anarchist literature itself), have been much less examined, analyzed, and debated than have developments such as socialist realism and other variants of Marxist or socialist literature.

Marxist critics, including Frederic Jameson and Terry Eagleton, have become well regarded and respected figures within the mainstream of literary criticism and their works key contributions to academic study. Even more, Marxist revolutionaries and activists, including most notably Lenin, Mao, Plekhanov, and Trotsky, have all been studied and discussed within academic and popular criticism, their works contributing to literary studies and literary theory over decades. The Marxist influences on well regarded and widely read authors as diverse as Bertolt Brecht, Jack

London, Victor Serge, and Ignacio Silone alike are well known and commented upon.

Such has certainly not been the case with anarchism, either at the level of literary creation or at the level of criticism and literary studies. There is no anarchist literary reading list and no consensus view on the subject of anarchist literature. Happily, however, there are beginning to emerge courses on anarchism and literature or anarchist literature. A shift is gradually taking place as a new generation of scholars, many awakened by the alternative globalization struggles of the late twentieth and early twenty-first century, turns to anarchism as a perspective for understanding the world and as a force for positively changing it.

Anarchist interpretations of literature and anarchist literary criticism are spread through, and touch upon, a range of sources, academic and popular — those with limited circulation and those more broadly distributed. At the same time anarchist critics have not brought their perspectives together in more extensive volumes, as have Marxist and post-modern critics. As well, it might be said that while topics such as the state, economy, family, sexuality, prisons and punishment, ecology, and, even, psychology have all been central subjects of anarchist thought and discourse, literature has received less systematic or extended discussion within anarchist theory and analysis. This is curious given the influence that anarchist philosophy and practice have had on literary creation, including the works of major figures of literature. Anarchist sentiments, influences, and tendencies can be found in a range of writers and texts, from the explicitly anarchist to those who would not identify, or be identified, as anarchist. At the same time over the last century there have been important contributions by anarchists in critically rethinking literary creation. Indeed, recent scholarship notes the important part played by anarchist ideas in the development of literary modernism and postmodernism alike (Antliff, 2001; Shantz 2010b; Weir 1997).

For many of this emerging generation of scholars, the previous forms and expressions of radicalism that came to prominence among the academic left, particularly various forms of Marxism, are ill suited to offering inspiration or analysis for contemporary movements or struggles. For others, the radical criticisms of Marxism that emerged within critical theories and eventually post-structuralism and postmodernism are also found wanting, especially given their tendencies towards fatalism, defeatism, detached individualism, and obscurantism.

Anarchists, unlike many Marxists, have tended to stay away from notions of economic determinism or base-superstructure models of literature or literary production. Anarchists have stressed literature as part of people's ways of understanding and acting upon, of changing, social relations. Experimentation in form and substance is valued as means by which people contest, challenge, supercede or destroy the old values, morals, and norms under state capitalist cultures, while developing new ways of relating, expressing, and viewing the world and people's place within it. Literature and culture, in addition to being made by political economy also remake political economy. Thus, while Marxist literature has tended to be dominated by socialist realism or "proletarian fiction," anarchist literature, notably, has perhaps disproportionally produced — and made real innovations in and contributions to — science fiction and speculative fiction.

Anarchists have often turned to the utopian novel as the means for expressing their visions of anarchist social relations and the form of possible worlds in which anarchy might be practiced. Anarchist author Paul Goodman notes the connection between science fiction or utopian literature and criticism. Utopian visions help criticism by offering an imaginable alternative. Why criticize if there is no way to imagine a different way of doing things? Goodman described himself as 'thinking up little expedients of how it could be otherwise':

> I tend not to criticize, nor even to notice, until I can imagine something that would make more sense. My expedients are probably not workable in the form I conceive them, and I certainly do not know how to get them adopted — they are utopian literature — but they rescue me from the horror of metaphysical necessity, and I hope they are useful for my readers in the same way. (Goodman 1971, 236)

Partly this reflects the fact that anarchist societies have been realized in the modern era for only brief periods of time or within the context of small-scale experimental communities or intentional societies. At the same time it reflects the anarchist impulse toward creativity and a preference for imagining positive alternatives rather than (but not instead of) simply focusing on negative aspects of current social life.

This does not mean that anarchists abandon the task of, or dismiss the importance of, detailing and documenting social ills and injustices as part of broader processes of ending those ills and injustices. Anarchist literature does much in attacking social problems openly and clearly. Rather, it means that the emphasis of anarchist writers is on raising the imagination, inspiring new worlds, new ways of being, of raising the necessary questions about what might replace the mess of capitalism. Notably, too, rather than presenting the anarchist (or anarcho-syndicalist or socialist) future as a problem free utopia in which all contradictions and antagonisms have been resolved, anarchists honestly and unflinchingly, as in works like

LeGuin's *The Dispossessed*, raise the problems confronting attempts at social transformation and the reconstruction of social life.

A key expression of the "scientific" aspirations of Marxist socialist theory is offered when Bertolt Brecht declares: "A Socialist Realist work of art lays bare the dialectical laws of movement of the social mechanism, whose revelation makes the mastery of man"s fate easier" (1973, 13). Anarchists have been far less inclined to seek dialectical, or other, "laws" of social movement in art or literature. For anarchists, the mastery of people"s fate is through human action and thought, not the workings of "social laws," the existence of which anarchists have been largely skeptical.

Similarly, while Marxists have viewed literary works as expressing "advances towards a continually stronger, bolder and more delicate humanity" (Craig 1975a, 13), anarchists have been less certain, always aware of the reverses and declines that can, and do, also emerge — particularly, it seems, following supposedly socialist revolutions. Anarchists have not followed Marxists in spending much time trying to devise a law of literary development (see Craig 1975b).

For anarchists the literary imagination is related to the social situation and changes in the situation or context will lead to changes in literature — but not in any direct or determined manner. Anarchist literature might be described in the manner used by the anarchist turned socialist Victor Serge in his description of the victimized poet Osip Mandelstam: "a subversive praise of the imagination, an affirmation of ungovernable thought" (1975, 437). Anarchism is the philosophy of ungovernability par excellence.

Anarchists share with some Marxists the concern with the human qualities embodied in the working classes and oppressed, their cultures, social relations, and social struggles. Anarchists emphasize working class language and speech, views, perspectives, and experiences. They draw upon the cultures of the working classes and oppressed. They defend against the imposition or naturalization of format and promote the vernacular and popular expressions, working class idioms and styles. Anarchists have stressed *how* one might write, how one might develop new forms of representation (beyond concerns for proper content).

Anarchists situate themselves within struggle (or are situated there by social relations). Their criticism is partisan and engaged. They are clear about their opposition to the current authoritarian order and do not take a detached, academic position. Instead they distinguish between those works that accept the existing conditions and those that seek to challenge them in content and form, style and substance. They prefer works that help people in struggle understand struggles and perceive alternative orders to those works that simply entertain or confirm the current state of affairs.

The impacts of literature are difficult to quantify. Literature's effects are usually not immediate or tangible directly, although in times of social transformation, of course, these effects can be dramatic, playing into a widespread sense of hopefulness, change, and renewal. Literature can move us to action, trouble our conscience, raise new questions, or open new experiences. All of this can inspire us to change the world. At the same time, we must not expect too much from it. We cannot be disheartened or despair of the failure of literature to halt atrocities, as many writers did when confronted with the horrors of World War Two.

For anarchists, literature is a tool, and every tool can become a weapon—if you hold it right. The intention is not to provide *the* anarchist perspective on literature. Neither is it to speak to all varieties and forms of anarchist literature, much less to cover all authors, works, genres or periods of anarchist writing. The hope is that this work will provide an opening—allowing the reader to understand anarchism and anarchist approaches to literature, and to appreciate the richness and vitality of anarchism as a complex and diverse approach to life.

The Marxist literary critic David Craig, in his classic collection *Marxists on Literature: An Anthology*, found it acceptable to exclude Jean-Paul Sartre and Raymond Williams on the basis that "neither man has unambiguously avowed Marxism" (1975a, 23). At the same time both men, despite their contributions to Marxist theory, have the seeming disadvantage of having shown "demurrals at some Marxist axioms" (ibid., 23). Such nuanced relations to ideas is almost required of anarchist writers in their approach to anarchism. Anarchists thus tend to be more agnostic, less doctrinaire. They are certainly more open in terms of who is invited to be part of the club. Anarchists are mostly concerned with the separation of art and the artist into distinct, privileged categories within an unequal division of labor in which the creative expressions of regular folks are diminished, discouraged or eclipsed in favor of the works of "professional artists" who are positioned as experts who produce art as commodities.

Many might still be surprised at the notion that there is any anarchist literature, or anarchist contributions to literature. Readers who doubt the artistic or social significance of anarchist literature should read the works of Ursula K. LeGuin, or reread Joyce or revisit Soyinka. The present work might best be read alongside those works. Some shared point of discussion might help to move us beyond the general dismissal, contempt, panic, and misapprehension that often accompany any discussion of anarchism within statist societies—particularly in the current period of "age of terror" moral panic over anarchist direct actions and black bloc property destruction during political protests. *Against All Authority* invites and encourages such rereading. It offers its own rereading of these authors and more. It examines in detail various expressions of the literary imagination and literary production within anarchism.

Anarchist literary work remains diffuse and diverse, contradictory and distinct. Anarchist criticism is sporadic, disjointed, tentative, unsystematic. The present work is not intended to be authoritative or a fixed statement on anarchist literature or criticism. It is rather a beginning of a conversation, a starting point for future, further discussions.

There is no other comparable work available that examines anarchism and literature within the context of anarchist social movements. *Against All Authority* addresses a substantial gap in the literature both in modern literature, and overlooked connections with anarchist perspectives, and in political theory and theories of contemporary cultural movements. Hopefully it will prove of great interest for students of literature, politics, sociology, communication, and cultural studies as well as being of use to activists and members of community movements for whom anarchism represents a vital living movement.

Chapter One

Writing the anarchist specter

Of secret agents and men called Thursday

Anarchism has long haunted the troubled sleep of authorities of various political stripes. The history of anarchism is marked by direct conflict with state institutions and their apologists. This history has given rise to powerful imagery and intense literary depictions of anarchists as phantoms, devils, and beasts. Among the most striking images from this history are the caricatures of black trench coat-wearing "bomb throwers" who owe their fame to a limited range of activities at the turn of the nineteenth century. The representation of the anarchist as fanatic or terrorist was produced, disseminated, and reproduced in novels such as Joseph Conrad's *The Secret Agent* and G. K. Chesterton's *The Man Who was Thursday* along with many others. For Victorian and Edwardian authors anarchism was a "nightmare," a mysterious, dark, menacing place in the center of modernity, in need of being infiltrated, its secrets prised open. These works continue to keep the myth of the anarchist beast in circulation. In the popular imagination the specter of anarchy still conjures notions of terror, chaos, destruction, and the collapse of civilization itself (Marshall 1993).

The reality, however, is that in the movement's long history few anarchists have ever engaged in terrorism or even advocated violence. The distorted characterization stems almost from the startling bombings and assassinations which arose from the despair of the 1890s and, especially, from the need and desire of authorities to discredit and destroy anarchist movements that threatened elite rule (ibid.). To be sure, anarchism has counted assassins and bomb-makers among its number, figures like Ravachol and Emile Henry during the nineteenth century and Leon Czolgosz who assassinated President McKinley in 1901. Some contemporary anarchists choose as an element of style to play up this image, dressing entirely in black and printing "zines" (self-published magazines) with such titles as "The Blast"[1] and "Agent 2771."[2]

At the same time, while anarchism has not been free of violence, anarchism has been largely a peaceful tradition throughout its history (Woodcock 1962; Marshall 1993; Kornegger 1996). The writings of people such as William Godwin, Pierre-Joseph Proudhon, Peter Kropotkin, and Elisée Reclus are moved by sentiments of mutuality, conviviality, affinity, and affection. Anarchist practical initiatives have been directed predominantly towards building new communities and institutions. Where anarchists have engaged in violence it has been carefully directed against economic and political elites and political masters. For the most part, the history of anarchism shows that it is anarchists themselves who have been subjected to political violence. As Peter Marshall (1993, x) notes, anarchism "appears as a feeble youth pushed out of the way by the marching hordes of fascists and authoritarian communists" (not to mention the hordes of nationalists and populists). When it comes to martyrs to state violence, anarchists, as for most working class and poor communities, have not been lacking. The Haymarket Martyrs, Joe Hill, Frank Little, Gustav Landauer, Sacco and Vanzetti, the Kronstadt sailors and the Maknovists of Ukraine are only a few of the anarchist victims of state violence.

There should be no surprise, of course, that rulers have always desired to construct anarchists as nihilistic fanatics, for anarchists question the very legitimacy of authoritarian rule itself. As Marshall notes, the radical implications of anarchism have not been lost on rulers (of the left or right) or ruled, "filling rulers with fear, since they might be made obsolete, and inspiring the dispossessed and the thoughtful with hope since they can imagine a time when they might be free to govern themselves." (ibid.) This chapter examines some of the distorted literary depictions of anarchists as expressed in prominent literary works particularly *The Secret Agent* and *The Man Who was Thursday*.

1   Originally the title of Alexander Berkman's newspaper of the nineteen-teens it has been adopted by contemporary anarchists in Minnesota for their own paper.
2   This was the code name assumed by the assassin and terrorist Sergei Nechaev, a colleague of Bakunin's and author of the notorious Catechism of a Revolutionary. Nechaev was the source for Dostoevsky's character Peter Verkhovensky in The Possessed.

On the Central Anarchist Council

Anarchists are invariably presented as hatching deadly plots against humanity or civilization (rather than against capital or the state—the real targets of anarchist organizing). Anarchists are represented as purveyors of terror and disorder—much as they are in the present period of neoliberal capitalist globalization. The anarchist is routinely described as carrying a bomb in his pocket. They are said to hate life itself—their own as well as that of others.

G. K. Chesterton creates an archetype of anarchism as the realm of the violent secret society in his classic *The Man Who Was Thursday*. For Chesterton's undercover officer Syme, revolt is merely revolting. It is akin to vomiting. Revolt is a type of insanity. Protest against revolt is a call for common sense. For Chesterton revolutionists are marked by "bewildering folly" (2007, 39). The serious anarchist is someone who would revolutionize society on his or her lawn, not someone who would engage in popular movements of the working class, poor and oppressed. The anarchist is an evil or distorted hobbyist. In the renderings of Chesterton and Conrad, to be "really an anarchist" is to use bombs (ibid., 8). When Rosamond Gregory, the anarchist's sister, asks secret agent Syme if he thinks her brother is really an anarchist, she asks: "He wouldn't really use—bombs or that sort of thing?" (Ibid.). As if the use of bombs marked the anarchist as an anarchist.

For non-anarchist writers of both fiction and non-fiction, particularly in the late nineteenth and early twentieth centuries, everything about anarchism is marked by secrecy and deception. Secrecy is a theme that runs especially through the Victorian and Edwardian accounts of anarchy. Anarchists are marked by what Syme calls "a scientific attempt at secrecy" (ibid., 17). Secret agent Syme is introduced to the literal anarchist underground when his table at the dim bar to which he has been taken by the anarchist poet Lucian Gregory drops down a secret chimney into a dark cellar below. At the bottom of the drop, Gregory gives a secret knock and password at a heavy iron door as means to gain entry. Inside the secret, hidden corridor the passageway gleams with ranks of handguns and rifles hanging from the walls. Through the passageway the men are delivered to a chamber filled with — what else for anarchists — "They were bombs, and the very room itself seemed like the inside of a bomb" (ibid.). This chamber of weapons is Gregory's proof to Syme that he is a "serious anarchist."

G. K. Chesterton and Joseph Conrad, authors of two of the most widely read fictional works dealing with anarchism, both held wild notions about anarchist organization. The anarchists of Chesterton's work belong to a nefarious European Central Anarchist Council, despite the facts that anarchists are decentralists. Anarchists were elected to the General Council of the Anarchists of Europe and held "official" papers to prove it. Chesterton describes a layered conspiracy, making a sly comparison to the church: "This is a vast philosophic movement, consisting of an outer and inner ring. You might even call the outer the laity and the inner ring the priesthood" (ibid., 46). The Central Anarchist Council, in Chesterton's rendering, even has a president, a positional designation that is, of course anathema for any anarchist.

The anarchist poet Gregory suggests that for the president of the Central Anarchist Council, "Caesar and Napoleon would have been children in his hands" (ibid., 20). The comparison to the heads of state is curious but then again so is the presence of an anarchist "president." The president, called Sunday, is referred to as "Bloody Sunday" by his admirers. Sunday was said to be possessed of an almost supernatural power. He was capable of striking Syme dead as if by magic. The president frightened Syme unlike anything on earth. The bloodthirsty image of the anarchist is played up in the nickname of the president. Strangely too the anarchists have a reverence, a fear, for their President Sunday.

For the anarchists, even thought was like a bomb. This is expressed by the Secretary, in his argument for the new method over the simpler and more direct form of the knife attack:

> 'The knife was merely the expression of the old personal quarrel with a personal tyrant. Dynamite is not only our best tool, but our best method. It is as perfect a symbol of us as is incense of the prayers of the Christians. It expands; it only destroys because it broadens; even so, thought only destroys because it broadens. A man's brain is a bomb,' he cried out, loosening suddenly his strange passion and striking his own skull with violence. 'My brain feels like a bomb, night and day. It must expand! It must expand! A man's brain must expand, if it breaks up the universe.' (Ibid., 67)

The Secretary is said to have a "white-hot enthusiasm unto death, the mad martyrdom for anarchy" (ibid., 101). The supposed bomb-throwing Marquis is presented as the devil itself. Syme sees his task as guarding the civilized world against hell. Yet when Sunday uncovers an officer in the ranks of the Council, he simply sends him on his way.

Anarchists are portrayed as amateurs playing the fool. Claiming to care about exploitation, there are few of the exploited among them. In other instances, anarchy is dismissed as mere childishness. The likelihood of an anarchist rising is viewed with great skepticism. Such turmoil could not be produced by children. They are said to seek destruction for destruction's sake.

The serious anarchist would revolutionize society on his or her lawn (Chesterton 2007, 7). The anarchist is merely a hobbyist—one with a dangerous, deadly hobby. They are not to be taken seriously in themselves, or for their politics, but only as a threat to decency and order. Anarchists are contrasted with the working people who "believe and obey" (ibid., 166). It is denied that working people could ever be anarchists—in complete disregard for the actual history of anarchism, a largely working class movement.

When the car, full of inspectors, crashes into a lamp post, the police attempt to escape the anarchists. The following exchange portrays the anarchists again as wanton destroyers of property:

> 'Well, we smashed something,' said the Professor with a faint smile. 'That's some comfort.'
>
> 'You're becoming an anarchist,' said Syme, dusting his clothes with his instinct of daintiness.' (ibid., 161)

Anarchist Gregory draws the distinction between order and anarchy in the comparison between a lamp (order), "ugly and barren," and a tree (anarchy), "rich living, living, reproducing itself" (ibid., 10). Here again, order is the human creativity of industry and civilization while anarchy is the unthinking wildness of nature.

Anarchists are said to be savage and solitary. For Chesterton anarchists are "a handful of morbid men, combining ignorance with intellectualism" (ibid., 40). Anarchy is described as a "philosophy of dirt and rats" (ibid., 166). Anarchists are "lawless little men" involved in "mad little movements" (ibid., 45). There is a certain amount of Orientalist fear in this too. The anarchists are described as a part of a fanatical eastern church of pessimism.

What do these morbid men, these fools who dare call themselves anarchists, want? For Victorian and Edwardian authors such as Chesterton and Conrad, it is largely a Nietzschean attempt to move beyond good and evil. In Chesterton's rendering:

'To abolish God!' said Gregory, opening the eyes of a fanatic. 'We do not only want to upset a few despotisms and police regulations; that sort of anarchism does exist, but it is a mere branch of the Nonconformists. We dig deeper and we blow you higher. We wish to deny all those arbitrary distinctions of vice and virtue, honour and treachery, upon which mere rebels base themselves. The silly sentimentalists of the French Revolution talked of the Rights of Man! We hate Rights and we hate Wrongs. We have abolished Right and Wrong. (ibid., 18)

The former Thursday of the anarchist council imagined by Chesterton is remembered as a "dear dynamiter" (ibid., 28). His contributions were lauded thus: "As you know, his services to the cause were considerable. He organized the great dynamite coup of Brighton, which, under happier circumstances, ought to have killed everybody on the pier" (ibid.). The term "dynamiters" even becomes a synonym of, a replacement for, the term anarchists in Chesterton's work. Anarchist groups are identified as dynamiters clubs. And, indeed, the Council members spent their time hatching plots to kill the czar or the president of the French Republic. How would they do it? By bomb, of course. Wednesday was to carry the bomb.

The anarchists are presented as enemies, not of the state, but of society — a significant distinction. Anarchists are represented as opponents of love, moral courage and ideals of "brotherhood and simplicity" (ibid., 31). Never mind the communal writings and emphasis on mutual aid and social cooperation of anarchist theorists such as Kropotkin and Reclus.

Such anarchist visions of positive social life, lived among people motivated by good will and shared sympathies are obliterated. The anarchist, ironically, is presented as the destroyer of worlds. In Chesterton, the accusation rings on the ears of the anarchists: "You can make nothing. You can only destroy. You will destroy mankind; you will destroy the world" (ibid., 166–167). Chesterton quotes *The Dunciad* against the anarchists:

Nor public flame, nor provate, dare to shine;
Nor human light is left, nor glimpse divine!
Lo! thy dread Empire, Chaos is restored;
Light dies before thine uncreating word:
Thy hand, great Anarch, lets the curtain fall;
And universal darkness buries all. (ibid., 163)

The anarchist Gregory is made to nod assent with this assessment: "'You are right,' said Gregory, and gazed all round. 'I am a destroyer. I would destroy the world if I could'" (ibid., 204). Anarchists are presented, quite simply and unambiguously, as the "great enemy of mankind, whose very intellect was a torture chamber" (ibid., 65). The police, on the other hand, are presented as pillars of "common sense and common order" (ibid.).

Chesterton's anarchist poet Lucian Gregory proclaims the lawlessness of art, the art of lawlessness. Anarchists live for the dramatic statement, the moment of infamy. In Chesterton's presentation the anarchists are not in it for the long haul of building social alternatives and changing society, despite the reality that most of anarchist history has been preoccupied with such social organizing efforts. In Gregory's "anarchist" vision:

> 'An artist is identical with an anarchist,' he cried. 'You might trans-
> pose the words anywhere. An anarchist is an artist. The man who
> throws a bomb is an artist, because he prefers a great moment to every-
> thing. He sees how much more valuable is one burst of blazing light,
> one peal of perfect thunder, than the mere common bodies of a few
> shapeless policemen. An artist disregards all governments, abolishes
> all conventions. The poet delights in disorder only. If it were not so, the
> most poetical thing in the world would be the Underground Railway.
> (ibid., 5)

In one passage the agent Syme makes his pitch to be elected as Thursday on the Anarchist Council. His winning appeal is telling in terms of how it presents the popular perception of what anarchists would support. Syme proclaims to applause:

> But I say that we are the enemies of society, and so much the worse for
> society. We are the enemies of society, for society is the enemy of
> humanity, its oldest and its most pitiless enemy (hear, hear). Comrade
> Gregory has told us (apologetically again) that we are not murderers.
> There I agree. We are not murderers, we are executioners (cheers).
> (ibid., 32–33)

Syme's affirmation of the stereotypes of anarchy is met with cheers by the anarchists. Rather than address or correct the slanders leveled against anarchists Syme calls on the anarchists to fulfill them, to make them real. Elevating his rant he urges:

> I do not go to the Council to rebut that slander that calls us murderers; I
> go to earn it (loud and prolonged cheering). To the priest who says
> these men are the enemies of religion, to the judge who says these men
> are the enemies of law, to the fat parliamentarian who says these men
> are the enemies of order and public decency, to all these I will reply,
> 'You are false kings, but you are true prophets. I am come to destroy
> you, and to fulfil your prophecies.' (ibid., 34)

The vision of the anarchist as nihilist is extended in a passage in which Syme speaks with a police officer. The officer, referring to the anarchist conspiracy's inner circle, relates to Syme the anarchist vision as he understands it:

They are under no illusions; they are too intellectual to think that man upon this earth can ever be quite free of original sin and the struggle. And they mean death. When they say that mankind shall be free at last, they mean that mankind shall commit suicide. When they talk of a paradise without right or wrong, they mean the grave. They have but two objects, to destroy first humanity and then themselves. That is why they throw bombs instead of firing pistols. The innocent rank and file are disappointed because the bomb has not killed the king; but the high priesthood are happy because it has killed somebody. (ibid., 46–47)

The anarchists had sworn to destroy not merely capital and the state, but the entire world itself. Thus the real aims and intentions of anarchists were themselves annihilated by the literary Victorians and Edwardians. Chesterton mocks anarchists, in a familiar caricature that persists to the present day, as killers of people but lovers of animals. Of the former Thursday it is said:

As you also know, his death was as self-denying as his life, for he died through his faith in a hygienic mixture of chalk and water as a substitute for milk, which beverage he regarded as barbaric, and as involving cruelty to the cow. Cruelty, or anything approaching to cruelty, revolted him always. (ibid., 28)

This was the "ear" of positivist criminology and the bizarre writings of the criminologist Cesare Lombroso, who claimed an ability to identify the "criminal type" by the shape of ears and the roughness of hands. With his sham "science" of phrenology, Lombroso asserted that criminals were an evolutionary throwback, a branch of the evolutionary tree that was not quite human. These missing links were so-called atavists — and they were identifiable to the trained eye. One of Lombroso's specimens of the criminal type was "The Anarchist" and he contributed an infamous article on the criminal anarchist. Both Chesterton and Conrad, in varying ways, invoke Lombroso (though Conrad, at least allows the anarchists a rebuke). The anarchists bear deviance in their bodies and faces. Something in each of them looks the dynamiter. For the most part they appear diabolical and grotesque. They mostly display "a demonic detail" (ibid., 59). In Chesterton's terms:

That lop-sided laugh, which would suddenly disfigure the fine face of his original guide, was typical of all these types. Each man had something about him, perceived perhaps at the tenth or twentieth glance, which was not normal, and which seemed hardly human. The only metaphor he could think of was this, that they all looked as men of fashion and presence would look, with the additional twist given in a false and curved mirror. (ibid.)

Anarchists are said to wear fanaticism on their faces, to carry it on their being. The president is, of course, a gigantic man, the enormity of his social threat borne in the enormity of his own physiognomy, in his body. So colossal and foreboding is the president that simply seeing him gives Syme a sense of drawing near to the "headquarters of hell" (ibid., 57). The anarchist poet Lucian Gregory affirms the Lombrosian suspicion in a burst of anarchist rage:

'My red hair, like red flames, shall burn up the world,' said Gregory. 'I thought I hated everything more than common men hate anything; but I find that I do not hate everything as much as I hate you!' (ibid., 205).

Chesterton describes one anarchist so: "It seemed as if all friendly words were to him lifeless conveniences, and that his only life was hate" (ibid. 53). This is a man whom inspector Syme has only just met. The inspector knows nothing of him. His face is otherwise described as dignified. Yet it must be that he is driven by hate. He is an anarchist, after all, for Chesterton. Anarchists are marked in their personages and in their thoughts as the threatening other. In Chesterton's rendering:

Each figure seemed to be, somehow, on the borderland of things, just as their theory was on the borderland of thought. He [Syme] knew that each one of the men stood at the extreme end, so to speak, of some wild road of reasoning. (ibid., 63)

At the same time, those who were not anarchists could be identified by their bearing or even their style of dress. The face, collar, and boots, and nothing more, of presumed anarchist Doctor Bull assured Syme that the good doctor was not an anarchist.

Occasionally the idea occurs to Syme that he is really only dealing with ordinary men with regular human frailties, such as age, nervousness, or short-sightedness. Such sympathetic sentiments always leave him rather quickly, however.

Of course, in the end every person on the dreaded Council ends up being revealed to be a police inspector. And this says much about the way in which the specter of anarchy haunts the already troubled minds of insti-tuted authorities and conventional wisdom. The fears they create and hold are really unrecognized images of their own construction of the world. A world of violence and disorder, inequity and injustice, that they them-selves maintain, create, and uphold.

Even the composition of the Council was a sign of Sunday's cunning. The police officer who shares with Syme the revelation that the Council is populated with inspectors responds thus:

> 'Mean!' said the new policeman with incredible violence. 'It means that we are struck dead! Don't you know Sunday? Don't you know that his jokes are always so big and simple that one had never thought of them? Can you think of anything more like Sunday than this, that he should put all his powerful enemies on the Supreme Council, and then take care that it was not supreme? I tell you he has bought every trust, he has captured every cable, he has control of every railroad line — especially of that railway line!' and he pointed a shaking finger towards the small wayside station. 'The whole movement was controlled by him; half the world was ready to rise for him. But there were just five people, perhaps, who would have resisted him … and the old devil put them on the Supreme Council, to waste their time in watching each other. Idiots that we are, he planned the whole of our idiocies! Sunday knew that the Professor would chase Syme through London, and that Syme would fight me in France. And he was combining great masses of capital, and seizing great lines of telegraphy, while we idiots were running after each other like a lot of confounded babies playing blind man's bluff.' (ibid., 136)

Even the revelation that Sunday himself is an officer does not settle accounts with the diabolical anarchists and the police must finally contend with Gregory, the true anarchist.

For the Victorian and Edwardian writers, working people were not conceived as anarchists or potential anarchists, despite the fact that they have typically made up the bulk of anarchist movements. Anarchists were usually portrayed as the enemies of regular folks — their message anathema to working people. Indeed, the police are certain that regular folks would rise up against the anarchists if the moment called for it. As Dr. Bull proclaims: "'If you really think that ordinary people in ordinary homes are anarchists, you must be madder than an anarchist yourself. If we turned and fought these fellows, the whole town would fight for us'" (ibid., 155). One of Syme's comrades declares:

> so you talk about mobs and the working classes as if they were the question. You've got that eternal idiotic idea that if anarchy came it would come from the poor. Why would it? The poor have been rebels, but they have never been anarchists: they have more interest than anyone else in there being some decent government. The poor man really has a stake in the country. The rich man hasn't; he can go away to New Guinea in a yacht. The poor have sometimes objected to being governed badly; the rich have always objected to being governed at all.

Aristocrats were always anarchists, as you can see from the barons' wars. (ibid., 141)

Sunday's associates were said to be South African and American millionaires. The inspector suggests that anarchists could never convert "any ordinary healthy person anywhere" (ibid., 142).

Secret agents

Joseph Conrad's account of anarchism in *The Secret Agent*, is based on an actual attempt by someone to blow up the Greenwich Observatory in 1894. Conrad viewed the work as a product of a period of mental and emotional reaction (1967, 7). He describes it as a tale of ugliness, of squalor, and sordidness (ibid., 8). As in other accounts of the day, the anarchists are portrayed as repulsive, worthy of scorn as well as pity. The anarchistic end is, for Conrad, one of "utter desolation, madness, and despair" (ibid., 12). For Conrad, the anarchists were simply, literally "lunatics" (ibid., 85). At the same time, he readily admits to having absolutely no contact with any real anarchists, even in passing. Yet he claims, perhaps in self-serving fashion, to have enjoyed a more concentrated purpose in writing it than any anarchist had in a lifetime.

In *The Secret Agent*, the main anarchist Verloc runs a seedy store, something of a porn shop, frequented by working class and poor males. It is suggested that, in the typical caricature of anarchists as slothful and purposeless, he spent much of his day lazing around, fully dressed, in bed. He was thoroughly indolent, his laziness itself described as, what else, fanatical (ibid., 20). In the view of Inspector Heat: "Not one of them had half of the spunk of this or that burglar he had known. Not half—not one tenth" (ibid., 86). Here Conrad shows too his contempt for working class activists and organizers: "He was too lazy even for a mere demagogue, for a workman orator, for a leader of labour" (ibid., 20). For Conrad, the suffering of poverty is dismissed as "the blind envy and exasperated vanity of ignorance" (ibid., 48). In his view, revolutionists, in the end, seek "the peace of soothed vanity, of satisfied appetites" (ibid., 73).

In all cases the priority is for the maintenance of ruling economic and political structures and relations, which are clearly threatened by anarchist movements and ideas. Property and luxury have to be protected "against the shallow enviousness of unhygienic labour" (ibid., 20). Again, working class organizers of all stripes are despised by Conrad. For Conrad, revolutionary reformers share the "temperamental defect" of disliking "all kinds of recognized labour" (ibid., 51). In his view: "The majority of revolutionists are the enemies of discipline and fatigue mostly" (ibid.). Their rebellion, if it can be called that, is waged against the cost in self-restraint and toil that must be paid for the supposed advantages and opportunities provided by the given social state. Fanatics simply view the price as oppressive or enormous. For Conrad: "The remaining portion of social rebels is accounted for by vanity, the mother of all noble and vile illusions, the companion of poets, reformers, charlatans, prophets, and incendiaries" (ibid., 52). Anyone, in other words, who might challenge the status quo, the taken for granted, the order of things.

Conrad shares with early social science writings on revolutions and rebellions the construction of protest as an outcome of individual motives and personal dissatisfaction. The specter of the isolated fanatic with a selfish grudge looms large. For Conrad: "The way of even the most justifiable revolutions is prepared by personal impulses disguised into needs" (ibid., 73). A figure of solitude who mistrusts humanity and views itself with a sense of superiority is described by Conrad as "the perfect anarchist" (ibid., 74). Inspector Heat, the officer dedicated to tracking down anarchists, does not know what anarchists want and he doubts that they do either. Of course, the discovery would have required actually listening to them or reading the ample and abundant materials that anarchists had already written and published at the time that *The Secret Agent* was being produced.

Once more the anarchist is excluded from being simply an aggrieved member of the working class, as one could never be part of the other in these constructions. All of humankind opposed them, even *other* thieves and mendicants, as if anarchists were simply or primarily thieves and mendicants (ibid., 85). Behind the police waited an invincible multitude arrayed against the anarchists. The anarchist stands in a "sinister loneliness" (ibid., 85). The lonely figure is haunted and pathetic. It was lonely not only because of the hideous vision it held to but because it was rejected by all others.

The fear of anarchy is summed up tidily by "the great lady," the wealthy salon host in *The Secret Agent*. In her view: "It appears we all ought to quake in our shoes at what's coming if those people are not suppressed all over the world" (ibid., 182).

As is the case with Chesterton's visions, the anarchists in *The Secret Agent* have leaders as well. Verloc was vice president of the group Future of the Proletariat. The anarchists are members of an always mysterious "red committee." There is even a Revolutionary International Council. In reality, in this case, the anarchist is actually a secret agent working for a foreign power. This is part of the mystery of anarchy, a representation of the secrecy and untrustworthiness of modernity.

Once again anarchists are imagined to desire a "clean sweep of the whole social creation" (ibid., 35). Blowing up a restaurant or theater is suggested as a lesson in revolutionary anarchism. Bomb throwing is again presented as the anarchists' "means of expression" (ibid., 36). Karl Yundt, "the terrorist," expresses his anarchist dream thus: "No pity for anything on earth, including themselves, and death enlisted for good and all in the service of humanity — that's what I would have liked to see" (ibid., 43).

Again, the crank criminologist Lombroso is invoked as a figure of science and his work is cited as the anarchists physically look the part of evildoer. All of the anarchists are physically repulsive, or even grotesque. They carry a menacing air. They are described as having an "expression of underhand malevolence" or "a moribund murderer" (ibid.). They are described as unhealthy looking with a lamentably inferior physique generally (ibid., 58).

For Conrad, anarchism "had more the character of disorderly conduct, disorderly without the human excuse of drunkenness, which at any rate implies good feeling and an amiable leaning towards festivity. As criminals, anarchists were distinctly no class — no class at all" (ibid., 85). Here Conrad makes a clever move. On one hand he takes an opportunity to reassert the claim that anarchists are not of the working class. They are a classless group, unrooted and shifting. This is a claim that sociologists have made about organizers of social movements in various eras. On the other hand he suggests that anarchists are a grim bunch, lacking good feeling and a festive spirit.

Again the lack of familiarity with anarchism is shown in the failure to appreciate the festive character of anarchism (and, indeed, of many anarchists). One might think immediately of Emma Goldman's famous quip, that got her into much trouble with some Marxists: "If I can't dance, it's not my revolution." Anarchists have long been dismissed by Marxists for being too festive, not serious enough in their politics and organizing. Conrad's lack of familiarity with anarchism is also shown in his refusal to recognize or admit the class character of anarchism.

Not only Lomboso is called into the discussion of anarchism but the figure of Herbert Spencer. The anarchists, despite all evidence to the contrary, are portrayed as Social Darwinists. The supposedly "anarchist" Professor is actually a Spencerite, who seeks a world where only "the fittest" survive—the complete antithesis of anarchism. The weak, he rails, are the "source of all evil" (ibid., 243). His prescription—a horror to real, living anarchists—is to exterminate them all. In the vile words of the Professor:

> They are the multitude. Theirs is the kingdom of the earth. Extermi-
> nate, exterminate! That is the only way of progress. It is! Follow me
> Ossipon. First the great multitude of the weak must go, then the only
> relatively strong. You see? First the blind, then the deaf and dumb,
> then the halt and the lame—and so on. Every taint, every vice, every
> prejudice, every convention must meet its doom. (ibid.)

This from a supposed anarchist. Never mind that Conrad's contemporary, and perhaps the most famous and influential anarchist of them all, Peter Kropotkin, devoted much of his intellectual research and publishing to detailed, historically and empirically informed, refutations of Spencer's work and all notions of Social Darwinism and "survival of the fittest." Indeed, Kropotkin's great work *Mutual Aid: A Factor in Evolution* is dedicated to illustrating the role of mutual aid and cooperation, rather than competition, in the development of animal and human communities. Alas, such are the misrepresentations that predominate within the non-anarchist literary portrayals.

The anarchists play upon what are called "sinister impulses" (ibid., 48). The bomb maker—the Professor—is described as cool, detached, uncaring. He is solitary. He is willing to give his explosives away to anyone who will use them. As he asserts: "The condemned social order has not been built up on paper and ink, and I don't fancy that a combination of paper and ink will ever put an end to it, whatever you may think" (ibid., 66). He has no time for propaganda by reason. His is propaganda by dynamite. This is the so-called "perfect anarchist." For him, only blood puts a seal on greatness. For the multitudes he has only contempt. The Professor is described in stark terms:

> And the incorruptible Professor walked, too, averting his eyes from
> the odious multitude of mankind. He had no future. He disdained it.
> He was a force. His thoughts caressed the images of ruin and destruc-
> tion. He walked frail, insignificant, shabby, miserable—and terrible in
> the simplicity of his idea calling madness and despair to the regenera-
> tion of the world. Nobody looked at him. He passed on unsuspected
> and deadly, like a pest in the street full of men. (ibid., 249)

And this is the menacing end of the novel. The Professor walking alone, unnoticed through the streets. The obscure but ever present threat of anarchist destruction. Overlooked but moving among us. The anonymous, mysterious character of modernity itself providing the means for his seclu-sion. Hidden in plain sight. In the anarchist dystopia of the Professor, only he remains — overlord of all the earth. In fact, his is actually the dream of capital — of the monopolist.

Anarchists and "red scares"

The image of the anarchist, especially the shadowy figure of the black trench coat-wearing bomb thrower that has persisted since the nineteenth century, brings together fears of disorder, social instability, and the threat of the outside agitator acting to undermine fundamental "democratic (read state capitalist) values" or, in the US context, the "American way of life." It might well be remembered that the first "red scare" in the US was actually directed at anarchist labor organizers during the last decades of the nineteenth century and first decades of the twentieth century. The 1880s saw a period of intense, and highly charged, public discussion of anarchism. This culminated in the passage in 1903 of an immigration law that sought to prohibit anarchists from entering the US (Hong, 1992). As Hong describes it:

> The anarchist was the constructed devil of the American civic religion
> of the late nineteenth century. It was made the bogeyman to guard the
> borders of the political allegiances, loyalties, and obedience of Ameri-
> can citizens. (ibid., 111)

The anti-anarchist "red scare" introduced durable, and easily manipula-ble, themes in American political life, not only as a justification for hege-monic ideologies and the construction of social cohesion, but also to delineate and to reinforce the acceptable features of American political culture (ibid., 110).

Notably, the anarchist specter has been especially prominent during peri-ods of great social upheaval and transformation such as the present period of capitalist globalization, characterized by the shift from the welfare state period of capitalism to the period of neoliberal capitalism. Similarly, the era of the first "red scare" was one of intense social conflict and cultural disloca-tion as traditional social relations and values were undermined or disman-tled. Under such shifting circumstances, forces striving for hegemony find themselves confronting the task of developing institutional and ideological strategies for forging some social consensus and cohesiveness, typically in the face of grassroots social and political movements seeking to establish forms of solidarity and social cohesion on their own terms. As Hong suggests:

> Lurking behind the attack on one kind of revolution of social relations was a different revolution: the appropriation and concentration of power in corporate capitalism and in the strong nation-state. A common interest with the ideology of the latter revolution was cultivated in inverse proportion to the anxiety created about the challenger. (ibid., 111)

As Hong illustrates, during the first "red scare" the image of the anarchist was deployed in a manner that prefigures the official response to anti-globalization movements today:

> The symbolic anarchist enemy came to personify the challenge of anti-capitalist ideas and values. It was constructed to evoke associations that fostered dependency on authority, freezing political perceptions and conceptions within an acceptable framework. By putting the 'anarchist beast' beyond the pale, it kept citizens within the fold. (ibid.)

Despite the claims of some commentators that the period of globalization has witnessed a declining role for nation states, it is more accurate to suggest that authorities within the present period, like the period of the first "red scare," have responded to social upheaval through the promotion of a strengthened national state and of values that support it.

As Hong (ibid., 110) suggests the "red scare" against anarchists, which marks the beginning of a modernist American political tradition, is significant "because it produced an evocative condensation symbol that has retrained its power into contemporary use. An excess of democracy can still be discredited as the threat of impending anarchy." The anarchist beast remains, even a century after it was supposedly first vanquished, a key ideological symbol in legitimizing state or corporate ideologies and practices, especially in the face of growing opposition movements against capitalist globalization.

As anarchists are quick to point out, such characterizations of activists and political movements will always be put forward by mainstream media regardless of the presence or size of any movement. In this they have clearly learned a lesson shared by cultural historians:

> The intensity of Red scares far exceeds the actual threat the scapegoat groups represent. This makes sense, insofar as the primary object of these campaigns is not to defeat the weak and resourceless enemy but to win favor for elements within the governing elite and to accomplish the ideological rearmament of a population. (ibid., 127, n. 4)

Such have been the motivations of the various "red scares" throughout history. Interests of power are also expressed in the literary distortions of anarchism. This speaks to the significance of honest engagements with and closer readings of anarchism and the literary imagination.

Conclusion

In her masterful and incisive meditation on political violence and assassination, Goldman turns to literature for key moments of reflection. She quotes the French novelist François Cappé on the psychology of the *Attentäter*, the assassin.

> The reading of the details of Vaillant's execution left me in a thoughtful mood. I imagined him expanding his chest under the ropes, marching with firm step, stiffening his will, concentrating all his energy, and, with eyes fixed upon the knife, hurling finally at society his cry of malediction. And in spite of me, another spectacle rose suddenly before my mind. I saw a group of men and women pressing against each other in the middle of the oblong arena of the circus, under the gaze of thousands of eyes, while from all the steps of the immense ampitheatre went up the terrible cry, *Ad leones!* and, below, the opening cages of the wild beasts.
>
> I did not believe the execution would take place. In the first place, no victim had been struck with death, and it had long been the custom not to punish an abortive crime with the last degree of severity. Then, this crime, however terrible in intention, was disinterested, born of an abstract idea. The man's past, his abandoned childhood, his life of hardship, pleaded also in his favor. In the independent press generous voices were raised in his behalf, very loud and eloquent. 'A purely literary current of opinion' some have said, with no little scorn. *It is, on the contrary, an honor to the men of art and thought to have expressed once more their disgust at the scaffold.* (Quoted in Goldman 1972, 211–212)

Goldman finds in Zola's works, *Germinal* and *Paris*, a profound insight into the character of those who turn to political violence as a response to social inequality and injustice. Zola's portrayals speak to the tenderness, kindness and sympathy for those who suffer that motivates those who engage in violence as a means to break a system of exploitation, misery violence and injustice. Goldman (ibid., 226) further notes the tribute of

Ada Negri, the Italian poet, to the anarchist Santo Caserio, whom she refers to as a sweet, tender plant, too fine and sensitive to withstand the cruelty of the world.

Goldman's essay "Prisons: A Social Crime and Failure" opens with a lengthy reference to Dostoyevsky's story "The Priest and the Devil" written in his prison cell in 1849. She then, after outlining some of the social harms of prisons, quotes Oscar Wilde's "The Ballad of Reading Gaol."

> The vilest deeds, like prison weeds,
> Bloom well in prison air;
> It is only what is good in Man
> That wastes and withers there.
> Pale Anguish keeps the heavy gate,
> And the Warder is Despair. (Quoted in Goldman 1972, 288)

Goldman finds a pathetic archetype in Archie, the victim in the novel *The Turn of the Balance* by Brand Whitlock. Archie, like so many real folks, was driven to crime by the cruel inhumanity of his environment and by the machinery of law itself (ibid., 290). Years before labelling theory would study the self-perpetuating character of labels applied by criminal justice systems, and the role of these systemic labels in reproducing criminal activity, Goldman identifies the role of the legal system and how it helps "to create the disease which is undermining our entire social life" (ibid.). Anarchists have had to struggle against and move beyond such labels while asserting their own perspectives on social and political change.

Chapter Two

Beyond socialist realism

The social theories of artistic production that have dominated the political left and progressive radicalism most broadly have been so-called social realism or socialist realism. These perspectives, to varying degrees, link artistic production with the developments of class societies, the needs of social change and the priorities of political organizations.

Anarchists share with Marxists a commitment to the working classes and oppressed — valorizing their perspective and experiences as a foundation for revolutionary movements for positive social change. Anarchists do not have, with socialists, "the problem of peaking for people at large in a way that is authoritative, the voice of the vanguard, while avoiding hectoring from on high" (Craig 1975a, 16). Anarchists have rejected the role of authorities or vanguards in other people's lives. They have also rejected the control of artistic production by political parties or political elites of all stripes. Thus, they have been critics of the expressions of social realism and/or socialist realism that have emerged within the authoritarian left.

Protest literature

Protest literature is often dismissed as utopian (or needlessly dystopian), romantic, naïve, or worse, artless. In his essay "Social Criticism," written at the beginning of the social upheavals of the 1960s, anarchist commentator Paul Goodman strikes a cautious note about the capacity of social writing to make a difference. At the same time he wonders why the forces of rebellion do not match the level of social troubles. Goodman explores the ways in which the literature of social criticism differs from social scientific analysis and reform politics.

Goodman notes that social criticism forms its own genre of literature. Among the satirists, like Voltaire and Mandeville one sees it, as in Rabelais and Cervantes. Goodman suggests that since the Industrial Revolution much of moral philosophy and sociology resembles social criticism. Goodman identifies this as a strain. In his view, this strain runs back to the writers of the French Revolution, particularly Voltaire, de Sade and Rousseau. In a time of complete dismay, they portray a situation in which a corrupt regime has corrupted all of humanity. Human nature, however, is not inherently corrupt and through enlightenment people can become rational and free. Not revolutionary, the emphasis is rather on pedagogy, reason, social science and economics after the revolution had occurred (Goodman 1994, 2). It stresses that political power is based on superstition and myth. It is morally bankrupt (ibid., 3). For Goodman, this strain survives through the nineteenth and twentieth centuries in the writings of anarchist radicals who advocate thoroughgoing revolution and social reconstruction through education, civil liberties and the decentralization of industry and administration at direct, face-to-face levels.

Goodman also identifies a strain of critique that runs back through the Reformation. In this literature, exemplified by Swift and Erasmus, humans are hopelessly irresponsible by nature. There the tone is one of detached dismay matched with humour. Human civilization is a disaster and will continue to be.

Protest literature is often "the vitality of the powerless" to use Goodman's apt phrase (ibid., 8). It tries to shame the shameless. It would make states and capitalists feel guilty or embarrassed simply for doing precisely what they need to do to thrive under a capitalist system — to pursue their own interests. The critic is the court jester of state and capital who keeps "clear before them the true, the good, and the beautiful as they do otherwise. He helps articulate and work off whatever self-contempt they feel. He provides the excellent entertainment of conversation-pieces" (ibid., 9). This can even assist the powerful and elites. Political handlers and public relations training serves to encourage even the most questionable powerholders to acknowledge their failings when called on them. As Goodman notes,

> For now the more sensitive and intelligent *know* they are morally bankrupt and they proceed like pure hipsters. It is only the utter stuffed shirts and horse's asses who can make public speeches with a good conscience as they roll on. (ibid.)

Now, as then, this remains perhaps the primary difference between liberals and conservatives.

Clearly radical artistic production must go beyond this. It must be more than simple criticism. The anarchist artist does not seek to shame those who have no shame. Yet questions remain about the relationship of radical political movements and artistic production. The most prominent response to such questions has come in the form of socialist realism.

Against "hard realism"

Explicit revolutionaries, like Karl Marx and many of his followers, have focused on changes in productive relations, believing such changes would encompass other changes. Less have Marxists questioned education, morals, aesthetics or technology. Art is to be a reflection of, and expression of, the structural changes occurring in class societies.

Marx and Engels, for example, chastise the socialist Lasalle for not placing enough stress on the plebeian and peasant elements in his drama. For Engels, the drama is a work of history, a representation of specific forces and relations, and he writes at length in his letter detailing for Lasalle the shifting balance of forces and the rise of peasant movement in the time of the play (during the decline of feudalism) (1975a, 210–212). Engels similarly criticizes Minna Kautsky and Margaret Harkness for a lack of realism in their respective novels. Harkness is condemned for failing to show the working class as a rising mass, instead portraying their passivity (Engels 1975b, 267–268; 1975c, 269–271). Yet, in the latter case, the representation of passivity, as one of the manifestations of working class life, is, in fact, a realist portrayal of specific activity under specific conditions.

In its harshest terms socialist realism has advocated that, for artists and writers, "their duty first and foremost is to understand and know the people well" (Mao 1956, 66). Mao went so far as to argue that writers who do not fulfill this duty produce works "without savour or sap" which "often contain awkward expressions of their own coinage which are opposed to popular usage" (ibid., 66–67). Contrast this with the anarchist inspired works of Hugo Ball, Ursula K. LeGuin or James Joyce who have challenged popular usage as a means to urge new ways of thinking about, challenging, and moving beyond existing social structures. For Mao, the corrective to such experimentation and individual idiosyncracies was that "all artists and writers of high promise must, for long periods of time, unreservedly and whole-heartedly go into the midst of the masses, the masses of workers, peasants and soldiers" (ibid., 67). This is the basis for what might be called a "hard realism." Such is the statist, authoritarian approach to art, in the view of anarchists. This is a moralistic approach that decontextualizes art and the artists, removing them from real conditions of production. It is a model stuck on a limited understanding of class ill-suited to life within advanced capitalist relations of production.

Even the Marxist Georgei Plekhanov sounds a warning about the utilitarian approach to art favored by government authorities:

> To conclude with this side of the question, I would say, in addition, that political authority always prefers the utilitarian view of art, to the extent, of course, that it pays any attention to art at all. And this is understandable: it is to its interest to harness all ideologies to the service of the cause which it serves itself. And since political authority, although sometimes revolutionary, is most often conservative and even reactionary, it will be seen that it would be wrong to think that the utilitarian view of art is shared principally by revolutionaries, or by people of advanced mind generally. (1975b, 278–279)

Unfortunately, Plekhanov was not as critical when it came to the place of literature within his own statist revolution. His description above would have provided an excellent assessment of art within the Soviet state.

Bolshevik leader Leon Trotsky gives the classic defense of statist socialism and communism. Trotsky identified the function of art in the needs of the working class which are in his view expressed in the form of the proletarian state. For Trotsky this goes beyond the force of the state — it is a force of history. In his view:

> The proletariat has to have in art the expression of the new spiritual point of view which is just beginning to be formulated within him, and to which art must help him give form. This is not a state order, but a historic demand. Its strength lies in the objectivity of historic necessity. You cannot pass this by, nor escape its force. (Trotsky 1975, 370)

Anarchists reject the proletarian state and the view it as an expression of working class unity or consciousness as Marxists contend. For anarchists the state is always an instrument of class rule, of the particular interests of those groups that direct the state apparatus. In the actually existing socialist states the Communist Party censored and harassed writers. They decreed what literature was once and for all. The styles and themes of a new literature were not those of artists inspired by and engaged with the people or the revolution (as in earlier stages) but rather those of the chastened, frightened, opportunistic. Artists were instructed in the format of the socialist authorities supposedly in the service of the motherland. Enforced conformism erased the artists' responsibility, to himself or herself as well as to society. The artist became a functionary, a bureaucrat. Or a prisoner. Or an exile. Or worse. Notably, it was anarchists such as Emma Goldman and Alexander Berkman who were among the first to warn the world (and the political left) about what was actually happening in the new Soviet society. Unfortunately, many on the left rejected them, attacked them, for their honesty.

One must always hold the memory of the numerous poets and writers tormented and killed under socialist regimes. Reflect on those shot for little more than expressing "openly counter-revolutionary opinions," the verdict against them based solely on the great judgment of some Associations of Proletarian Writers (Serge 1975, 437). The massacres of Soviet writers represented "one of the fundamental events of culture" in the twentieth century (ibid., 438). Many of the founders of Soviet literature were simply assassinated. Of course the real list of writers lost to the Party is not fully known. Victor Serge suggests that young revolutionary writers, after the Revolution, disappeared in the thousands (ibid., 439).

Serge provides important insights into the psychology of the socialist state, and those subject to it, despite taking a less critical position towards it that have those commentators who maintained their anarchist principles:

> It is allowed to publish a great poem of love. It is mortally forbidden to ask of the state what has happened to poets and prose writers who have disappeared. Even love must hold its tongue on the threshold of dungeons. (ibid., 438)

The attempt at erasure of the literary imagination by Soviet authorities was totalistic. Once the authors fell from favor their very existence was annihilated. This socialist realist approach is, despite revolutionary platitudes, the antithesis of revolutionary perspectives within anarchistic approaches to the literary imagination and literary production.

Serge notes too the complicity of socialists outside the Soviet Union in erasing the condemned from histories of Soviet literature. Too often were they overlooked or passed over without comment (either to their works or their passing). Such was the context that confronted Goldman and Berkman in their efforts to warn the left what was happening so that the situation might be changed before it was too late. Of the failure of socialist intellectuals, Serge remarked:

The poet is suddenly stripped of his clarity. 'What is truth?' asked Pontius Pilate of the condemned. Thousands of men formed by the intellectual disciplines of scientific thought — it seems — reply in fact: 'It is the commandment of the Leader of my party.' This is the death of intelligence, the death of ethics. (ibid., 443)

Incredibly, despite the histories of Stalinist misery to which he himself surrendered his work, the Marxist theorist and critic Georg Lukács suggests that literature based on angst, as in Franz Kafka, no matter how artistic, cannot avoid *objectively* "guilt by association with Hitlerism and the preparations for atomic war" (1975, 384). For Lukács, critical realism provides the theoretical link between communities of opinion "and the creative process itself" (ibid., 384). Anarchistic writers like Kafka represent for Lukács "an aesthetically appealing but decadent modernism" (ibid., 394). This is an accusation leveled against many anarchists by Marxist communists who deride the anarchist attack on all instituted, including communist state, authorities. For Lukács, another anarchistic author, James Joyce, whose works are discussed at length in a following chapter, was merely an uninvolved spectator of his era (ibid., 389).

For anarchists, this is not particularly surprising, sad though it is. Anarchists have always warned about the dangers of political parties and the allegiance to parties and party authorities over principles and personal liberty. Thus anarchists have mobilized against political vanguards of the left and of the right.

Beyond literary determinism

Anarchists have not followed Marxists, such as Georgei Plekhanov, in locating specific artistic forms in the specific development of the productive forces (Plekhanov 1975a, 84). For Plekhanov art is determined by the production forces, including the content of art (ibid.). According to Leon Trotsky, literature is merely the representation of a new class. In his view:

Literature, whose methods and processes have their roots far back in the most distant past and represent the accumulated experience of verbal craftsmanship, expresses the thoughts, feelings, moods, points of view and hopes of the new epoch and of its new class. One cannot jump beyond this (Trotsky 1975, 376–377).

Indeed.

Anarchists do jump beyond this, of course, in viewing literature as a contested field, even in its emergence in new epochs, among various sectors of the working class and oppressed. Anarchists point out also that too often, rather than expressing the hopes of a new revolutionary class, socialist literature has expressed the desires of a ruling class in formation.

For anarchists critical discussions of present-day material reality alone cannot "enthuse the human soul" (Goldman 1972, 99). Goldman rejects economic determinism and vulgar representations of class struggle. Economic factors are, of course, important, even fundamentally so, in understanding social development. Yet this is not enough to understand social change, much less revolution or rebellion. No single factor in individual or social behavior can be called "the factor of decisive quality" (ibid., 99).

So too does Goldman reject economic determinist visions of creative production, literature and art. Her criticism holds for realist movements and approaches to art. For Goldman, Marxism has failed in overlooking "the human element" (ibid., 100). For Goldman: "Important as the economic factor is, it is not enough! The rejuvenation of mankind needs the imagination and energizing force of an ideal" (ibid.). Goldman asserts: "But only narrow and willful deprivation can persist in remaining blind to the important role played by an idea as conceived by the imagination and aspirations of the individual" (ibid., 99). Following Nietzsche, who greatly influenced her thinking, Goldman argued that literature, rather than propagandizing, or representing reality in a proper way, must instead encourage a "transvaluation of accepted values" (ibid., 127). Anarchists realize that peoples' vices and follies often give real satisfaction. They are not the expressions of the fallen. There is no talk of "bourgeois decadence" in anarchist literature, as there has been in the Marxist literature. Indeed anarchist literature has often been associated with so-called decadent literature.

Anarchists have been willing to take on such accusations, suggesting that critical perspectives and analysis came be sparked in even the least likely genres. In speaking of romance and love—topics given little attention or concern by most socialist militants—Goldman admits her preference for romantic flights of heart than the correctness of political novels:

> Rather would I have the love songs of romantic ages, rather than Don Juan and Madame Venus, rather an elopement by ladder and rope on a moonlight night, followed by the father's curse, mother's moans, and the moral comments of neighbors, than correctness and propriety measured by yardsticks. (ibid., 141)

Thus, she is critical of the rather stilted portrayal of the emancipated professional woman in Jean Reibrach's novel *New Beauty*, in which a young woman physician is unable to express her feelings for a young man. She remains a model of liberated sexuality — exact, rational and well behaved. For Goldman, a portrayal entirely lacking in imagination or force. Such depictions keep the ideal representative from drinking from the fountain of life (ibid.).

The anarchist transformations in social commentary would not be done solely through dry social, or socialist, realism, through diatribe or a didactic approach to discourse. Rather, anarchist literature would make use of satire, humor and sharp wit. As Paul Goodman (1994, 7) suggests: "If a society suffers from glut, ritual, and greed, destructive ridicule *is* positive." Goldman argues that in modern America such approaches are lacking. Her criticism is apt in the twenty-first century as it was in the twentieth. Popular discourse is dominated by cliché and distracting silliness in the service of corporate conglomerates and media monopolies. In her day, only the muckraking journalist offered any of the popular critical discourse of which Goldman speaks.

Intellectuals too have wandered from the public stage. In place of public engagement many have retreated into the comforts of specialization and the safe careerism of tenure. For Goodman (ibid., 2), much of satire is limited to the invective of a loyal opposition that accepts the existing state and/or social structure but condemns specific governments or parties. Muckraking is more outraged and expresses its outrage at all parties and can verge toward the revolutionary.

At the same time anarchists should avoid the dreariness of slogans that mark too much activist art. Slogans, despite the hopes of those who raise them, tend not to inspire. Neither do they linger in the memories of those who hear them (as opposed perhaps to those who recite them). The best radical literature always seeks something more. As Paul Goodman notes:

> Slogans can't last long in either common speech or literature. In agitated situations, the new people, making bad literature (and sometimes even writing it down), always recall ancient languages, as the Reformers picked up the Hebrew patriarchs, the French Revolutionists picked up Marcus Brutus, the radical students pick up Marx, and the Hippies pick up various Indians and Amerindians; but the good writers ridicule these too. (Goodman 1971, 241)

Anarchists have long suggested that much leftist writing lacks vitality. It does not stir the imagination. For DIY anarchist writer Professor Calamity:

> So much of the far left political writing lacks a heart; it's so cerebral now. I feel like the anarchists of the past had more heart than many of my comrades today. Anarchists may be smarter than they were in the

> past, but they miss the human connections that can make our isolated
> scene a real movement. (Quoted in Killjoy 2009, 74)

Anarchists typically avoid the heroic and opportunistic portrayals that
characterize much socialist realism. Resistance is not a matter of heroism
but of everyday life. It is a matter of survival for the poor and oppressed.
Anarchism shares with existentialism this recognition that times and peoples' experiences of them are often bleak. That despite this people
resist—not as heroes, but often in humble, understated ways. Unlike
socialists, such as Marx and Engels themselves, who criticize artists for
failing to depict the working class or peasantry in vital, heroic struggle,
anarchists are often less optimistic in assessing peoples' options or opportunities in a given period. For Professor Calamity:

> I feel fiction should present some human truths and the truth is that
> most of us will *not* succeed even if we are smart and struggle hard, but
> that doesn't diminish our cause. In a sense, it's optimistic to think that
> people will stand up and fight back even when they are going to lose.
> That's something that is lost in most American fiction. (ibid., 76)

Anarchist literature does not need to lie to people or deceive them to make
things seem easier or more certain than they are.

Anarchists recognize that communication can readily become, as in
Vygotsky, "the internalized ideology of the State" (Goodman 1971, 214).
By nullifying the choice of speakers—their individuality, their free
action—their thoughts become internalizations of top-down institutions
(ibid., 213). In such a system it may be possible to do away with the individual speakers themselves. Such has been the fate of too many authoritarian socialist projects.

Anarchists speak against socialist realist notions of communication.
They reject the notion that the artist can know the essential character of a
class or social group which they can reveal. Anarchists do not accept
Marxist notions of false consciousness, in which the understandings of life
held by working class and oppressed people are viewed as mistaken or
incorrect if they are not explicitly revolutionary. Anarchists recognize that
people make choices within specific, often negative, contexts. Decisions
reflect strategic choices, often survival choices. Less than revolutionary
choices are not necessarily wrong or false. The writer cannot be so arro-
gant as to claim that they can reveal the truth of struggle to people, to provide correct consciousness, which is the claim of much socialist realism. As
Paul Goodman suggests:

> If the speakers are free agents, we cannot know them through and
> through. What they do is probably not arbitrary, but *their* causes are

outside the speech event and partly outside of the realm of signs altogether. It is not possible to tell beforehand what sentences will be 'meaningful' for communication. It is possible, even frequent, that it is some unnoticed nuance or connotation of the signs, or a fleeting gesture, even a 'misunderstanding,' that in fact communicates, rather than the common code or the prefabricated representations. (ibid., 221–222)

Such is the case no matter how much the artist might wish to express "underlying laws" or the "objective needs of the class" or "the Party."

Conclusion

At the same time, anarchists have not been romantics objecting only to the vulgarity of bourgeois society and its excesses without objecting to bourgeois social relations themselves. They have not sought in literature an escape from the tedium and conformity of bourgeois culture. They have not opposed the symbols and styles of bourgeois culture while leaving the structures unchallenged.

For anarchists, art must have the courage to reveal and challenge the great social problems of any period. It must use a sharp, critical edge to expose and condemn social wrongs and demand fundamental changes to social life (Goldman 1972, 127). Tastes, pleasures, and desires are closely related to social conditions. They change as conditions change, but not, of course, in exact correspondence. Impressions change with changing conditions. Different ideas emerge and are sustained in different ways under different conditions. Practices of hegemony work to silence or distort those ideas that contextualize power, that encourage new ways of thinking and being against those ways preferred by power holders. Such has certainly been the case in the mistreatment of anarchy.

Anarchist literature suggests that the utopian and practical, the romantic and realist can find shared expression. More, it asserts the potency of art and refuses the call to sacrifice the imagination to the demands or supposed needs of material necessity or representationality. Anarchists, against the calls for social realism, affirm the coincidence, the unity of form and content, means and ends.

For anarchists, it is more realistic to situate artists and artistic production within specific existing social relations. Under such a view artists and their production can be seen to have their own proletarian character as part of capitalist labor markets and commodity cycles. Artists do not need to go to the proletariat in an external, moralizing process of conversion. Rather they are already proletarian in character (though the specific character of their work differs from other proletarians as the work of the factory auto assembler differs from the Wal-Mart greeter or fast food chain server). The task of the anarchist is not to moralize or chastise but rather then to analyze and organize. For anarchists, art and literature must struggle precisely against this sort of enforced notion of form.

Chapter Three

Anarchy against format

Socialist realism is an example of the conversion of radicalism into format. Paul Goodman makes the distinction between format and colloquial speech as an important aspect of anarchist literature. By format, Goodman means imposing a style on the literary that is extrinsic to it (1994, 109). For Goodman, the dictionary definition of format is quite telling.

> **Format.** — n. **1.** the shape and size of a book as determined by the number of times the original sheet has been folded to form the leaves. **2.** the general physical appearance of a book, magazine, or newspaper, such as the type face, binding, quality of paper, margins, etc. **3.** the organization, plan, style or type of something: *They tailored their script to a half-hour format. The format of the show allowed for topical controversial gags.* **4.** *Computer Technol.* the organization or disposition of symbols on a magnetic tape, punch card, or the like, in accordance with the input requirements of a computer, card-sort machine, etc. — *v.t.* **5.** *Computer Technol.* to adapt (the organization of disposition of coded information) on a magnetic tape, punch card, or the like, to conform to the input requirements of a computer, card-sort machine, etc. (Quoted in Goodman 1994, 109)

Not only does format have no literary power, but in the end it destroys literary power, co-opting it and taking the life out of it. Editors chop sentences and paragraphs simply to fit word lengths. Assistant editors rewrite sections because they need to justify their job. Writers are asked to simplify arguments because the publisher has a low opinion of the readers' comprehension levels. These are some of the things that Goodman (ibid.) identifies as effects of format. All of these are impositions of format that place functionality above content or style.

The impacts can be extensive and severe. As Goodman (ibid., 111) argues: "But by format, even without trying, it can kill feeling, memory, learning, observation, imagination, logic, grammar, or any other faculty of free writing." Format drains meaning from speech. As Goodman notes,

this can be done through high art, as in Proust, not only through bureaucratic dryness. In Goodman's view, format is particularly disastrous for
common or colloquial styles (ibid. 109).

Entire university disciplines break unique writing styles to make them fit
the format of the discipline, constraining creativity and expression in the
service of an arbitrary attachment to tradition and uniformity. In the name
of what? Science? Objectivity? Neutrality? This is an issue that I examine in
Chapter 10, "Autoethnography: writing an anarchist sociology?"

I can recall many such disciplinary impositions of format in my own
intellectual and academic experience. Growing up as a working class
youth in working class school environments, elementary and secondary,
there I experienced or witnessed many attempts to break students of their
colloquial, community, styles, modes and means of expression. So frustrated did I become that I began to write critical works directed against
these attempts to constrain and limit students' thinking and writing. My
essay "The Educational Suppression of the Abstract Mind," for advanced
level English, may have been my first anarchist essay. The teacher, more
sympathetic than some, found it well placed.

During my times as an undergraduate, by then at a prestigious institution, one of the leading in Canada, I encountered similar attempts to
impose format, though justified more according to the needs of specific
academic disciplines. During my second year, in the context of an experimental psychology class, I was reprimanded for using inappropriate language for a lab report. There I was told explicitly that the writing style,
apparently flowery and flowing, might have been suited to a course in Literature, but certainly would not do for Psychology. Having read many
Psychology journals, I am now sure that they were probably right. Such is
reading Psychology. Unfortunately this seemingly minor incident, a note
on a lab report, had a nearly disastrous effect on my writing. For a considerable time, I found it extremely difficult to write anything. What I did
write lacked confidence. I consciously sought not to be flowery or flowing.
The playful freedom that marked "The Educational Suppression of the
Abstract Mind" was being strangled, suffocated, even as the suppression
was becoming more thorough.

The consequences are clear. For Goodman:

> Obviously, the effect of format is worse if the writer must adapt him-
> self and write, rather than just having his writing mashed. Since writ-
> ing is inherently spontaneous and original, a writer cannot produce
> what is not his own without a broken spirit. (1994, 109)

Yet too many social pressures serve to compel or encourage format.

Format and hegemony

Paul Goodman and the anarchist linguist Noam Chomsky both note that under modern liberal democracies it is not feasible for states to rely on lies and propaganda for communication purposes. Speech cannot be controlled in the manner of totalitarian regimes and, anyway, brainwashing is less dependable than fear and panic, as critical criminologists have long pointed out. Instead, rulers within liberal democracies must "manufacture consent" (to use Chomsky's phrase). Part of the manufacture of consent — getting subject populations to go along with elite rule — is the broad deployment of format, the return to conventional, restricted expressions.

Format is not like the censorship that attempts to silence or erase speech, and is, because of this fact, much more insidious and difficult to contest (Goodman 1994, 110). Censorship, in its attempt to remove speech, can render it valuable, important. This, is turn, empowers speech — as is the case under all totalitarian regimes in which samizdat becomes highly sought after and appreciated (ibid., 110).

Neither is format like pure propaganda in telling lies or crass fabrications. Format uses speech in ways that mask the character of that use. Format presents speech as valuable, even respected, as in academic disciplinary conventions, while de-valuing and disrespecting it. Format deploys speech in specific ways for specific, functional and instrumental, purposes. At the same time it limits and restrains speech that is not properly "in form." As Goodman suggests:

> Rather, authority imposes format on speech because it need [sic] speech, but not autonomous speech. Format is speech colonized, broken-spirited. It is a use of speech as social cement, but it is not like the small talk of acquaintances of the street in their spontaneous style; it is a collective style for a mass. So in appearance it is often indistinguishable from the current literary standard. But in actual use it is evident from the first sentence that it does not tell anything. (ibid.)

The rendering of reading and writing as format is characteristic of any authoritarian (including state capitalist) society. This is so even where "the style of literacy happens to be the standard literary classics" (ibid., 112). In

authoritarian societies, mandarin literacy is affirmed as the way to succeed, to get by, to "make it." It is viewed as right and good (ibid., 112).

Contemporary mass media, anarchists have long noted, are particularly
beholden to, and productive of, format. As massive investments of capital,
they pursue primarily the sale of media time and space, constructing programs or articles such that they allow the proper ration to the advertisements. In Goodman's view:

> This sometimes produces heat, never light, usually nothing. It is a for-
> mat. What is glaring in the whole enterprise is the almost entire lack of
> will to *say* anything, rather than just provide a frame for the ads. (ibid.,
> 110)

Seeking a mass audience—the real commodity being traded in mass
media—the media product "must be sensational enough to attract many
and bland enough not to offend any" (ibid.). This can discourage writing,
particularly for those who write along lines of class, or whose styles are
rooted in less favored language.

Format and education

For anarchists, the love of literature is not nurtured in the institutions of
work and training. Anarchists advocate a literary approach to writing
(and teaching writing) in trying to encourage writing from the
student-learner's spontaneous, indigenous speech (Goodman 1994, 112).
Emma Goldman follows Emerson in saying that people are students of
words, but are shut up in schools and colleges where they gain little more
than a memory of words. For anarchists, learning can be much more.

Decades before Michel Foucault gained notoriety for the analysis,
Goldman noted the shared functions of school, prison and workshop. In a
manner strikingly similar to the postmodern theorist, Goldman argues the
carceral nature of schools. As she suggests:

> It is for the child what the prison is for the convict and the barracks for
> the soldier—a place where everything is being used to break the will of
> the child, and then to pound, knead, and shape it into a being utterly
> foreign to itself (Goldman 1972, 116).

Art, literature and drama, were of course, subjected to great censorship
during the time of Goldman's writings. Yet, such censorship, at school lev-

els, is still in operation today. One can still identify regular instances in which books are removed from the curriculum for fear that offence might be given to someone. Even more striking are the examples of the Texas School Board decisions in which works are rewritten, even at the expense of distorting history, to preserve conservative dogma or the ideological requirements of conservative social visions. One might also add the decision, in 2011, to rewrite *Huckleberry Finn* to make the language "less offensive" and more marketable.

The means for transforming common speech into format is, according to Goodman, to browbeat someone with verbal explanations that they cannot understand (1971, 212). For Goodman: "The way of breaking the spirit of a writer is to pay him to write what makes no sense to him in a style that is not his own" (ibid., 213). Such is the case in the corporate writing industries, and mainstream media, as in the "Party writing" of socialist movements. The anarchist Kropotkin offers an alternative approach. For Kroptkin, as Goodman notes: "You can teach anything to a child or an unlearned peasant *if you yourself* understand it concretely and therefore can follow *his* understanding and offer it by the right handle" (ibid., 212, emphasis in original). The responsibility is, thus, shifted from the student to the teacher.

Anarchist art and literature are not part of a scholastic or academic practice. Reflecting on his own youth, Goodman relates the following:

> I remember how at age twelve, browsing in the library, I read *Macbeth* with excitement; yet in class I could not understand a word of *Julius Caesar*, and I hated it. I'm pretty sure this is a common pattern. The survival of the humanities would seem to depend on random miracles which are becoming less frequent. (ibid., 47)

Anarchists point out that "reading and writing spring from speaking, our human way of being in the world; that they are not tools but arts, and their content is imagination and truth" (ibid., 111). For anarchists, reading and writing are engaged by children where they are interesting and relate to their personal lives and touch what they want to say themselves. They pursue writings that connect where they are rooted, even while uprooting them.

In recent educational systems in capitalist liberal democracies, format has been shaped by supposed labor market considerations, which come to dominate all levels from primary to post-secondary. Literacy is overtaken by credentialism and the training of specific mechanical skills or basic competencies. Sometimes not even that.

For Goodman, a sharp critic of bureaucratic schooling and pedagogical practices:

> It is likely that school-teaching destroys more genuine literacy than it
> produces. But it is hard to know if most people think that reading and
> writing have any value anyway, either in themselves or for their use,
> except that they are indispensable in how we go about things. (ibid.,
> 111)

Schooling renders reading and writing a type of format. This is done often
without any relation to the teaching and learning of reading or writing. A
format is "an imposed style with no intrinsic relation to good speech"
(ibid.). Goodman quotes the Soviet pedagogical theorist L. S. Vygotsky as
suggesting that it is actually necessary to destroy the natural style of students. For Vygotsky:

> In learning to write, the child must disengage himself from the sensory
> aspect of speech and replace words by images of words. It is the
> abstract quality of language that is the main stumbling block to learn-
> ing to write, not the underdevelopment of small muscles ... Our stud-
> ies show that a child has little motivation to learn writing when we
> begin to teach it. Written language demands conscious work ... The
> concrete totality of traits [must be] destroyed through abstraction;
> then the possibility of unifying traits on a different basis opens up.
> Only mastery of abstraction enables the child to progress to the forma-
> tion of genuine concepts. (Quoted in Goodman 1994, 112)

The implications are profound and far-reaching. The outcome, perhaps
paradoxically is not democratization or expansion of literature, but the
further specialization and exclusionism of literature and literary production. In Goodman's words:

> With us, as school reading and writing cease to have literary meaning,
> university study of Literature ceases to be about human speech,
> speech in its great examples. (It is a nice question, what university
> English studies *are* about.) And as fewer people read authentically,
> on-going literature may well become one of the minor arts, for con-
> noisseurs, like rose gardening or weaving. (ibid.)

People refuse and resist the language of schools. They do not willingly, at
first anyway, adopt its literary styles. Adolescents are perhaps most sus-
ceptible to format — the capture of their creative expression by format — using the language and tone of pop culture, advertisements and
subcultural style dominated by consumer marketing strategists, focus
groups and public relations campaigns. Of course, even then it is played
with, converted, subverted or, as for the Situationists, détourned. Speaking of Western liberal democracies, Goodman suggests:

> There is a kind of style to our speech. Its is the style of urban confusion: a Yiddish that chews and can assimilate the ads, the sociological jargon, the political double-talk, the canned entertainment. (ibid., 114).

There is, however, and this is a point of great importance for anarchists, resistance. People do challenge, oppose, confront, and coopt format.

Colloquial resistance

The forces of format can dominate and debase public discourse and literary styles alike. For many anarchists, resistance to format is expressed forcefully in colloquial speech. It is in colloquial speech, and the preservation of colloquial speech that many anarchists find the most promising potential for linguistic resistance to format. Of course, anarchists also stress material resistance to format, as we will examine in a following chapter on do-it-yourself literary production. According to Goodman:

> But colloquial speech is quite impervious to corruption by format. It has an irrepressible vitality to defy, ridicule, or appropriate. It gobbles up format like everything else. There are too many immediate occasions, face-to-face meetings, eye-witnessings, common sense problems, for common sense to be regimented. People who can talk can be oppressed but not brainwashed. Modern cities are depressing and unhealthy, but the people are not mechanical. (1994, 113)

For Goodman, colloquial speech shows both resistance and the difficulty of resistance. It is always an aspect of struggle, as are other social contests within state capitalist cultures. As Goodman suggests:

> The deep pathos of colloquial speech—with its indestructible good sense, eye-witnessing, communal vitality, and crotchetiness (including much private error and deep-rooted tribal prejudice)—is that in highly organized societies its field of operation is strictly limited. We can speak good colloquial where we have freedom to initiate and decide. When our actions are predetermined by institutional and political frameworks that are imposed on us, we necessarily become anxious, unconfident of ourselves, and we fall into institutional and ideological format and its mesmerized thoughts. Thus in our societies there is continually spoken a dual language: Intimately, people talk sense — about politics, the commodities, the schools, the police, etc. — yet they also talk format, and act on it. In totalitarian societies, where a

> strong effort is made to reform colloquial speech to official format, the effort cannot succeed, but people do begin to whisper and fall silent; finally, only a few brave writers, who have a very special obligation to honourable speech, continue to talk like human beings. (ibid., 114)

Goodman supports the Wordsworthian view that "uncorrupted common speech heightened by passion and imagination, binds mankind together" (1971, 230). It can have more to recommend it than the utilitarian speech of liberals or the ideological speech of radicals (ibid., 230). Goodman reflects on his own use of colloquial and literary expression:

> My reliance on colloquial speech and the process of literature is certainly closely related, whether as cause or effect, to my political disposition. I am anarchistic and agitational, and I am conservative and traditional. So is good speech. (ibid., 240)

Colloquial speech connects with the anarchist emphasis on disruptive play. For Goodman:

> Insistently and consistently applied, any humane value such as common sense, honor, honesty, humor, or compassion, will soon take one far out of sight of the world as it is; and to have meaning is one of the virtues that is totally disruptive of established institutions. (ibid.)

Colloquial speech is often anarchic. As Goodman notes:

> Colloquial speech cannot be regimented, whereas even perception and science can be regimented — perception because it is solitary and passive, science because they can put blinders on it like a directed horse. But the vulnerability of the colloquial, we saw, is that its freedom is limited to where the speakers have initiative, eye-witnessing, and trust, and these limits may be narrow indeed. But the literary process expands these limits by historical memory, international culture, and welcoming the dark unconscious which common folk prudently inhibit. (ibid., 240–241)

Anarchists are aware of, and try to fend off, the tendency of youth or new social movement activists to take on the language of rebellion, opposition and activism as a format — to repeat catchphrases and assertions in the manner of truisms or groupthink.

In western societies, the colloquial is not generally engaged with the literary. This can be unfortunate in making both less clear, incisive, and forceful than they might be. It can also limit the capacity of each to expand its range of expression and circulation. It can limit the conversation.

Der Einzige: the unique

Many anarchists share with artists the emphasis on individual uniqueness as "a most potent factor for individual endeavor, for growth, aspiration, self-realization" (Goldman 1972, 50). Certainly such an emphasis drives the famous work of the proto-anarchist champion of individualism Max Stirner. This view is most forcefully expressed in his great book *Der Einzige* ("The Ego and Its Own"). This marks them as distinct from much of socialist perspectives on art and literature. At the same time anarchists emphasize the social instincts — the factors of mutual aid, solidarity and collective or communal well-being. This marks them as distinct from variants of liberalism and the liberal emphasis on the abstract individual.

For Goldman, "[t]he very essence of individuality is expression" (ibid., 88). Individuality is an aspect of growth and development that cannot be accounted for by reference to the group. At the same time, for anarchists, individuality is not the mechanistic (or legal) "individual" of mass or statist society. Individuality is also not the same as the "individualism" of Social Darwinism and economic *laissez faire*.

Individualism is the restraint of individuality, for anarchists. It is the conversion of life into a race for externals, possessions, prestige or status. This individualism, and its "devil take the hindmost" approach to inequality, is the justification for slavery, injustice and class domination. Under this individualism, political tyranny and social exploitation are upheld as virtues (ibid., 89). Attempts to gain freedom are denounced as threats.

Anarchists suggest that writers do not need to be inventive stylists. Most will not be. They will use a mix of standard, traditional, or other available styles. For Paul Goodman:

> Good style does not need to be novel, but it must be genuine, coming from how the writer is, speaking his animal cries, squaring with what he sees, not avoiding the others, not censoring. It is his colloquial speech, but more artful. And since the common style of any going culture is always a viable hypothesis, it might be a writer's own, with little new in it. (1971, 195)

What Emma Goldman called the "genius of man" — another name for individuality — actually breaks dogma, custom, and taboos. It defends against conformity, censorship and authoritarianism. Yet, anarchists suggest, this individuality has only showed its most wonderful results when strengthened by co-operation with other individualities (Goldman 1972, 95). As Goldman suggests:

> Socially speaking, the criterion of civilization and culture is the degree of liberty and economic opportunity which the individual enjoys; of social and international unity and co-operation unrestricted by man-made laws and other artificial obstacles; by the absence of privileged castes and by the reality of liberty and human dignity; in short, by the true emancipation of the individual. (ibid., 97)

As Goldman's quote makes clear, the emancipation of the individual is a *social* or collective emancipation involving the abolition of laws, states and the caste and class relations upon which they rest and which they preserve. By anarchism, Goldman means "the philosophy of a new social order based on the released energies of the individual and the free association of liberated individuals" (ibid., 100). The pioneers in literature remain alive to their times. Those that compel their times to accept them, as in Zola and Tolstoy, find support in emerging groups seeking new visions and new social truths (ibid., 178). Changes in social environment produce changes in psychology that impel new movements in art. Changing the world is a part of creative growth and development. It is part of the artistic process.

In the end, Goodman sums up the power of literature:

> It provides me a friendly community across ages and boundaries and cheers my solitude. I join in. Writing is not boring. It is the way I pray to God and my present community. As a writer I am patriotic — democratic — legitimate as the royal family — and to be meaningful I rebel (1971, 241–242).

Literature is both much less and much more than the social realists and propagandists would have it.

Chapter Four

Intellectual proletarians

Anarchists have developed analyses of creative workers that move beyond liberal notions of "the artist" as a privileged figure whose work is somehow beyond the materiality of everyday labor relations. For anarchists, the artist is not a privileged figure who works in isolation from social relations to produce works of individual genius. Rather the artist is an intellectual worker — or intellectual proletarian, to use the term preferred by Mikhail Bakunin and Emma Goldman — whose work is situated within specific production relations and who owes much to the social knowledge of the society and its point in history.

The intellectual proletarian, like the manual worker, is separated from the very things s/he produces. There is little personal contact with the industry in which they are employed and they are strangers to the processes of which they have been rendered little more than mechanical parts (even if the most important or necessary part). Intellectual proletarians also lack self-direction. Material considerations and social prestige take precedence. The free choice of voluntary, independent thought and activity is restricted for most.

Anarchists make the point that at this period in time, almost everyone, excluding a very narrow class, has become proletarianized. Proletarianization goes well beyond manual or industrial labor, encompassing the great diversity of spheres of activity throughout society. It is not an effect produced solely by the assembly line. As Goldman (1972, 176) suggests: "in the larger sense all those who work for their living, whether with hand or brain, all those who must sell their skill, knowledge, experience and ability, are proletarians." Most intellectual proletarians are actually existing in conditions of much precarity, dependent upon elites for sustenance as are manual workers, but more vulnerable to the labor market given the time and resources invested in their profession and the specific character of their skills and training. In an earlier work, Goldman suggests that what she calls the intellectual proletarians, like workers in shops and mines are subjected to an insecure existence, dependent for their

livelihoods upon the owners of capital. She suggests that the intellectual proletarians are in some ways more dependent given the subjective character of
their work, the whims of taste and fancy and their general unpreparedness for
other forms of labor.

The social condition of the intellectual proletarian

While the intellectual proletarians in theater, art, universities, and colleges
can, of course, draw a greater income and enjoy fame and lifestyles that
elude the manual worker, as well as having better working conditions, the
intellectual proletarians remain dependent upon the publishers, theatre
owners, galleries and newspapers. They also rely on the corporate constructions, and changing fads, of public opinion and preference. For
Goldman:

> This terrible dependence upon those who can make the price and dic-
> tate the terms of intellectual activities is more degrading than the posi-
> tion of the worker in any trade. The pathos of it is that those who are
> engaged in intellectual occupations, no matter how sensitive they
> might have been in the beginning, grow callous, cynical and indiffer-
> ent to their degradation. (1972, 177)

Even so-called success by such means, under such conditions, dampens
the creative passions. For Goldman, eventually, over time, such corrup-
tion, dulls one's senses and scruples, so that even those who begin with
lofty intentions cannot maintain or achieve transcendent creativity. They
struggle to produce a critical expression beyond market dictates. For
many, the goal is "making it" or "arriving" as artists. This becomes an
overarching consideration that comes to dominate the artist and her or his
art. This is also not surprising given the nature of survival under capitalist
economies in which people lack the access to resources and decision-
making channels necessary to determine the character of their own life
chances and opportunities. The uncompromising and daring often do not
"arrive" — in art as in life under state capitalism.

   This speaks as well to the nature of artistic authority and the separation
of artistic producers and consumers of art that reflects the broader separation of producers and consumers within capitalist economies generally.
The separation of creative producer and creative consumer, under a capitalist division of labor has privileged the artist as a special kind of pro-

ducer, an expert in the areas of culture. Anarchists challenge the separation of people into producers and consumers and also the emergence of the artist as a special or privileged social position. Why should people look to artists as *the* cultural producers, as the authorities in matters of culture, rather than become cultural producers themselves or valorize their own cultural production? In Goldman's perspective:

> Instead of that, we look to the artist, the poet, the writer, the dramatist and thinker who have 'arrived,' as the final authority on all matters, whereas in reality their 'arrival' is synonymous with mediocrity, with the denial and betrayal of what might in the beginning have meant something real and ideal. (1972, 177)

Yet, for Goldman these assumptions regarding the place of the artist must always be vigorously challenged. The relationship is more one of mutuality than is often supposed. In her view:

> The truth is, the people have nothing to learn from this class of intellectuals, while they have everything to gain. If only the intellectuals would come down from their lofty pedestal and realize how closely related they are to the people! But they will not do that, not even the radical and liberal intellectuals. (ibid., 180)

There are, of course, enormous pressures on authors to write the things that will sell, and which public taste will find palatable. There remains pressure to temper one's thoughts and write according to conventions and familiar forms. Even more, such restrictions constrain the political artist or intellectual beholden to parties or leadership cadre, whether conservative or communist. Thus anarchists are equally critical of art in the service of realism — determined by the preferences of political apparatuses, even, or particularly, where they claim to be vanguards of a new society in the making. For Goldman,

> those who are placed in positions which demand the surrender of personality, which insist on strict conformity to definite political policies and opinions, must deteriorate, must become mechanical, must lose all capacity to give anything really vital. (ibid., 177)

Thus the anarchist criticism of political authority extends to art in the service of political authority. The question is one of authority and the character of authority and, for anarchists, once again, means and ends must coincide.

Even movements for change create their own environments for "making it" or "arriving." Artists and writers can achieve what is sometimes called "subcultural capital," the street cred, rebel chic or hipness of the "outsider" artist or political artist. This can reproduce tendencies for sameness and derivative approaches to creative work. In real political movements the favored artists, the ones whose works are chosen for the posters, flyers, press releases and poetry readings are the ones who have "arrived" or achieved a level of subcultural in-group acceptance, rather than those who offer the most creative, challenging or, certainly, unique works.

Contemporary literature has been removed from community life, from workaday worlds. Still, there are attempts to substitute for this. Literary speech has been given over to political actions, as in guerilla theater or political songs or socialist realism or, more recently, political hip hop and punk, or alternative videos. As Goodman suggests:

> That is, the process of literature is not used in its natural power to find meaning and make sense, so that we can act in a world that has meaning and sense. It is claimed that there is no time for this; there is too much suffering and injustice. And only by engaging in revolutionary action can one produce new thought and lively words. (1971, 218)

This impetus can (and certainly has) too readily given rise to format, to stale, unengaged repetition. As Goodman notes:

> But in practice, I have found, this comes to not questioning slogans that are convenient for an immediate tactic or a transient alliance. The writers tell half truths. 'Action' becomes idiotic activism. The vocabulary and grammar are pitched to a condescending populism, about at the level of junior high school, including the dirty words. The thought is ideological through and through. By a 'revolutionary' route we come right back to format. (ibid., 218)

This has been the sad fate of too many political movements and activist subcultures. It is already noticeable in the narrow style and rhetoric of the alternative globalization activists, particularly in North America, with their hip-hop soundtracks and poster art. Complete with a profusion of the dirty words.

This is again a function of the separation of producer and consumer and the tendency to promote the artist as a special authority even within alternative or social change movements. It is one reason that anarchists suggest there are no leaders in the movement because everyone is a leader (or artist or organizer).

The artist who "will not worship at the the shrine of money" will not have to "wear other people's political clothes" (Goldman 1972, 178). This holds similarly for the radical artist who, while rejecting the shrine of money, would seek recognition and confirmation in acceptance by the political classes. The anarchist artist, holding to a courageous passion "will not have to proclaim as true that which is false, nor praise that as

humanitarian which is brutal" (ibid., 178). Here Goldman turns to the figures of the western artists who praised the Stalinist regime in Russia even
as she reported vividly on the repression she had witnessed first hand
under the Soviet regime.

Solidarity among proletarians

In the twenty-first century, a range of theorizing has posited the growing
significance of intellectual labor, creative labor and the growing centrality
of so-called immaterial labor within circuits of exploitation under
cyber-capitalism. Autonomist Marxist Michael Hardt, as one notable
example, highlights the ways in which contemporary capital relies on the
creative capacities of working people in the use and development and circulation of social networking and web technologies. The need is for solidarity between intellectual and manual proletarians, against the very
separation and division that create them as such. For Goldman:

> It is therefore through the co-operation of the intellectual proletarians,
> who try to find expression, and the revolutionary proletarians who
> seek to remould life, that we in America will establish a real unity and
> by means of it wage a successful war against present society. (1972,
> 185)

In Goldman's view, "though the intellectuals are really proletarians, they
are so steeped in middle-class traditions and conventions, so tied and
gagged by them, that they dare not move a step" (ibid., 183). Even where
they show sympathies for labor, and even where they are genuine in doing
so, the intellectual proletarians often remain distant, aloof, detached.
Sometimes they deceive themselves into believing that they contribute to
the prestige or legitimacy of the struggle (ibid., 181).

The difficult place of the creative worker under capitalism prompts
Goldman to ask:

> Under such a state of affairs, what becomes of the high mission of the
> intellectual, the poets, the writers, the composers and what not? What
> are they doing to cut loose from their chains, and how dare they boast
> that they are helping the masses? (ibid., 180)

For Goldman, works like Upton Sinclair's *The Jungle* do little to move a
hair on the head of companies like Armour meat packers, but do provide

the author with a tidy living and fine reputation. Even then, though, the author's following works cringe before respectability in hopes of finding a market (ibid., 182).

For Goldman:

> Strikes, conflicts, the use of dynamite, or the efforts of the IWW are exciting to our intellectual proletarians, but after all very foolish when considered in the light of the logical, cool-headed observer. (ibid., 183)

In some cases, of course, a sympathy emerges, where the issue is blatant enough or the injustice particularly, uncontroversially, grave. Sympathy does not provide the basis for an organic relationship among equals however. For Goldman (ibid., 183–184): "But the sympathy is never strong enough to establish a bond, a solidarity between him and the disinherited. It is the sympathy of aloofness, of experiment." It is the sympathy of those who still live in conditions of relative comfort and privilege or who are not immediately affected by the outcome of the struggle. In Goldman's view:

> The intellectual proletarians who are radical and liberal are still so much of the bourgeois régime that their sympathy with the workers is dilettante and does not go farther than the parlor, the so-called salon, or Greenwich Village. (ibid., 185).

Only when the intellectuals break with traditions, when they realize that society rests upon deceptions — and name them openly — and only when they give themselves to new ways, do they become a forceful factor in struggle, for anarchists like Goldman. Only when they repudiate wealth and status and refuse to serve the market.

Speaking of Russian intellectuals in the period before the revolution, Goldman suggests: "They went among the people, not to lift them up but themselves to be lifted up, to be instructed, and in return to give themselves wholly to the people" (ibid., 184). This accounts, in her view, for the heroism of the literature of the time and the unity between writers and the people. Such has been the case in the literature of various countries. For Goldman, it explains the strength of the Strindbergs and Mirbeaus.

Co-optation and format

The intellectual proletarians must "love the ideal more than their comforts," in the words of Goldman (1972, 185). For the sake of the crucial issues of the day, they will need to sacrifice external success. Of the social critic or protest artist in contemporary state capitalist societies it can be said:

> Their cultural dismay is genuine, but they take much too lightly the absence of initiative, morale, or commitment; their tone has neither indignation nor Utopian aspiration; they seem to be reconciled to people having no *souls*, in Aristotle's simple sense that the soul is self-moving and initiating and goes toward its good. (Goodman 1994, 8)

For Goodman, the conscious response to format — even confrontation with format — is avant garde. Here what is key is not the newness of what the writer is doing, but rather that an effort is being made to be different, not traditional.

Sometimes audiences can be lost or bored, even where the artist tries to be as clear as possible. The artist takes the current style for granted and does not intend to shock, yet powerful art may remain incomprehensible. Such is not the case for the avant garde. As Paul Goodman suggests:

> *Avant garde* artists do not take the current style for granted; it disgusts them. They do not care about the present audience; they want to upset it. Instead of trying to be as clear as possible, they are just as pleased to be incomprehensible, *fumiste* or *blageur*. A sign of success, or success itself, could be to provoke a riot. (1971, 216)

The provoking of riots has been a very real outcome for avant garde artsists, including for anarchists like Luis Buñuel.

Avant garde tends not to leave lasting works since the artist is too devoted to effect (Goodman 1971). At the same time, avant garde art is not free from the threat of co-optation. As Goodman notes: "But in a confused society, *avant garde* does not flourish very well. What is done in order to be idiotic can easily be co-opted as the idiotic standard" (ibid., 217). One can certainly call to mind some of the worst moments in punk, as in hip-hop and the hippie counter-cultures, as ready examples. Co-optation is always a threat. This is perhaps especially so where idiocy is involved.

For Goodman: "As a style, *avant garde* is an hypothesis that something is very wrong in society" (ibid.). This speaks to the common ground that has often been found between radical political movements and avant garde movements in art and culture.

Within capitalist economies there is room for sensationalism or "shocking art" — and it will even win major awards and state and corporate funding — that fails to challenge social relations or structures. Indeed, such works are needed as they open new areas and venues for commodification and innovation which can be sold back to the titillated public now attuned to and desiring the "shock" (rendered non-threatening). Sensationalism or shock become necessary commodities in a competitive mass media environment in which difference, where it can be safely incorporated, becomes a competitive advantage.

Such has been the lamentable fate of much of punk rock. Punk culture's initial capacity to shock, outrage and challenge advanced capitalist culture, has become a staple feature of advertizing, film and video games as well as graphic novels and reality television, in a culture in which rebellion is part of pre-conceived public relations schemes and brand "identities." Matched with a saleable emphasis on detached cool and cynical opportunism and the rebel's utterances are set to become the corporate jingle and theme song. This marks too the shift of early punk from movement (of movements) to subculture.

The force of conservatism will ensure reactions against artistic convention and moral repression. For Goldman (1972, 185): "Struggling artists, writers and dramatists who strive to create something worthwhile aid in breaking down dominant conventions."

Contemporary society is "dedicated to procedure and format rather than function and meaning" (Goodman 1994, 6). The pressures of format provide constant challenges that must be confronted in overcoming hegemonic ideological practices in state capitalist contexts.

Chapter Five

An in-between socialism?

Reflections on Joyce's idiosyncratic politics

Until very recently, most commentary on Joyce stressed that his works are apolitical. Since Joyce is said to have been largely apolitical it is claimed his work is also apolitical. More recently however some scholars have begun to look at the political, even radical, influences on Joyce and his engagement with radical political movements. While most of the commentators who have discussed Joyce's politics identify his influences as socialistic, it is more precise to suggest that Joyce's politics were influenced by libertarian versions of socialism, notably anarchism and syndicalism (or revolutionary unionism).

Significant works such as Dominic Manganiello's *Joyce's Politics* and Richard Ellmann's *The Consciousness of Joyce* have made a strong case for the Joyce's libertarian socialism. Landuyt and Lernout (1995) note that Joyce drew much of his research material for *Finnegan's Wake* from the anarchist geographer Lev Metchnikoff's masterwork *Les Grandes Fleuves Historique*. In preparing his notes, Joyce also gave particular attention to the "Introduction" written by the renowned anarchist geographer Elisee Reclus. A look at those instances where expressions of political concerns appear in Joyce's work suggests that there is a strong affinity with anarchist themes. Heyward Ehrlich notes that from the vantage point of the turn of the late twentieth century "we may easily forget to what extent late-nineteenth century and early-twentieth-century socialism and anarchism were necessary stations for the avant-garde on the road to literary modernism" (Ehrlich 1997, 84).

Other commentators, such as Robert Scholes suggest that Joyce exhibited a general disillusionment with socialism that affected many exponents of European modernism. Scholes suggests that the failings of mass socialist parties, eventually culminating in their capitulation at the outbreak of World War One, which saw socialists supporting their national bourgeoisie in war efforts, brought "authoritarian and totalizing proclivities" within socialism to the fore (Scholes 1989, 29). In the case of Joyce these tendencies, according to Scholes, "took an aesthetic direction toward the artist as a supreme figure, absolute in his own world and without any specific social responsibility" (ibid.). A more recent work, James Fairhall's *James Joyce and the Question of History* (1993) also provides a portrait of Joyce as a youthful enthusiast who later became disillusioned with socialism. Noted theorist Helene Cixous, in *The Exile of James Joyce* (1972), goes even further in condemning Joyce for a perceived authoritarianism. For Cixous Joyce enjoyed only "two socialist years" which simply served as "a mask for the 'inner heroism'" and "'redeeming selfishness' of the artist" that represented his true political values (Cixous 1972, 202–203).

In my view such approaches, which read Joyce's politics through the lens of traditional socialist categories are not suited to understand the complexity of Joyce's idiosyncratic political vision. Joyce's notions of the artist as heroic herald of a new world, rather than standing counter to socialism invoke visions of socialism that, despite their marginalization from the mainstream of socialist politics, were vital during Joyce's lifetime. As only one overlooked example, I would argue that the emphasis on the artist as mythic herald of a new world, is an already present characteristic of the Sorelian revolutionary syndicalism which influenced so strongly Italian syndicalists and anarchists, and through them, Joyce as well. According to Caraher,

> a fuller, more detail-oriented, social construction of Joyce's politics, as enacted through his life and texts, tends to place the author's European modernism not so much within the camp of international socialism ... as on its intellectual fringes (Caraher 1999, 176).

Any discussion of Joyce's politics must avoid simplifying his complex ideological impulses despite the many interpretive challenges they pose.

Partly Joyce stands counter to the orthodox socialism by which he is usually measured. Instead Joyce suggests an anti-feudal rather than anti-capitalist socialism based not on the industrial proletariat, from which Joyce experienced and felt some distance but rather from a déclassé petty bourgeoisie, an "in-between class" that painfully felt the constant threat of downward mobility and impoverishment.

> The conventional working class—gardeners, plumbers, carpenters—has virtually no representatives here. Joyce's people belong almost exclusively to the lower middle class, often affecting a sense of superiority that is only a reflection of their own insecurity. Poised

> between upper-class aspirations and the possibility of descent through
> the no-safety-net floor of 1904 society, Joyce's characters inhabit a gap,
> a site of high anxiety in historical Dublin. (Sherry 2004, 8)

Joyce evokes a complex variant of socialism which finds its inspiration and
speaks of the concerns of overlooked classes, those who do not play the
world historic part of either the proletariat or the bourgeoisie in the dominant Marxist versions of socialism. In looking at Joyce, the socialist vision
or unity is opened to significant, if under-appreciated counter or marginal
currents within the history of socialism. Closer attention to Joyce's socialism reveals the complex and contradictory forces of radical modernism as
well as hinting at alternative visions of social struggle which cannot be
contained within binaries such as "socialism or barbarism" that inform the
works of critics such as Robert Scholes. In this way a re-thinking of the
sources and expressions of Joyce's socialism provides a useful starting
point for re-thinking the sources and influences underlying European
modernism as well as opening interesting avenues for understanding histories of socialism.

Colin MacCabe (1979) argues that a reading of Joyce's correspondence
with his brother Stanislaus between 1905 and 1907 suggests a powerful but
highly personalized interest in revolutionary socialism. For MacCabe, the
letters reveal fundamental concerns and influences that further account
for contradictions in Joyce's politics.

> In these letters we can read the contradiction between an optimism
> engendered by Italian socialist politics and a pessimism confirmed by
> the developments of Irish nationalism. Joyce's politics were largely
> determined by attitudes to sexuality. Central to his commitment to
> socialism was his ferocious opposition to the institution of marriage,
> bourgeois society's sanctified disavowal of the reality of desire.
> (MacCabe 1979, 160)

In this chapter I discuss these aspects of Joyce's politics to highlight the
complex and heterodox character of the socialist vision he develops.

Sherry suggests that a touchstone for the development of Joyce's political sensibilities can be found in the figure of the Irish syndicalist James
Connolly. For Sherry, Connolly provides both a parallel as well as a contrast for Joyce's socialism. Connolly eventually arrived at an uneasy settle-
ment between socialism and Irish nationalism in which nationalism was a
useful expedient in arriving at socialism. For Connolly, nationalism could
contribute to social regeneration only insofar as it served to separate the
Irish from the interests of the English aristocracy. In this way nationalism,
by fomenting the spirit of separation from the imperialist bourgeoisie,

might contribute to a process of class rebellion that would eventually supercede it.

While Joyce at times allows for an uneasy acceptance of Irish nationalism he elsewhere maintains that an English presence in Ireland might contribute a necessary part to the evolution of socialism (Joyce 1966). Specifically, English investment would contribute the capital required for industrial development and the corresponding emergence of a full-fledged organized working class. This view, however misguided, fits with a certain Second International version of socialism that argued capitalism, and the superceding of feudal relations, was a requisite part in the transition to socialism.

Perhaps more sympathetically, Sherry suggests that this acceptance of an English presence invokes Joyce's pan-national view of socialism and his hope that the new century might usher in the end of international war (2004, 10–11). This hope was, of course very soon dashed on the rocks of 1914. As Stanislaus Joyce recounts, in describing his brother's socialist leanings: "My brother thought that fanned nationalisms, which he loathed, were to blame for wars and world troubles" (1958, 85).

Connolly's expression of socialism, tinged with nationalist sentiments, can be said to reflect one crucial fact of Irish social history at the time — the absence of a mass industrial proletariat. For Connolly nationalism served as a necessary addition to socialist ideology given the absence of a broad and united proletariat that might play the role assigned to it by Marxism.

For his part, Joyce was as aware as Connolly of this aspect of the Irish social context and saw the necessity of revising orthodox socialism in light of this. In his letters Joyce offers the conclusion: "The Irish proletariat is yet to be created" (1966, 174). From this crucial fact of history, Joyce drew much different conclusions. For Joyce the very lack of a mass industrial proletariat in Ireland suggested the appropriateness of an anarchist rather than a socialist (or Marxist) program of social change.[1]

Sherry suggests that this awareness was central to the socialism of Joyce's younger years which developed from his youthful experiences and peaked in 1906–1907 during his time in Italy. Joyce's stay in Rome coincided with a meeting of the international socialist congress. As Sherry notes:

> Among the rival factions at the congress he prefers the trades-unionists or Syndicalists, who subscribe to an anarchism Joyce justifies in

---

1 These readings also provide an alternative perspective from recent work such as Emer Nolan's *James Joyce and Nationalism* (1995).

view of the problems peculiar to Irish social history, in wording that
forces to a focus the predicaments underlying Connolly's own argument and rhetoric (Sherry 2004, 10).

In response, Joyce contemplates the necessity for "the overthrow of the
entire present social organisation" in order to spur "the automatic emergence of the proletariat in trades-unions and guilds and the like" (ibid.). In
this Joyce echoes popular revolutionary syndicalist doctrines of the day
which argued for the revolutionary general strike as the mythic force
which might regenerate the working class and its organizations through
the heroic form given to their struggle. Indeed French syndicalists as well
as Italian insurrectionary anarchists (both of whom played a part in the
Rome congress) advocated the general strike as the means by which an
unformed or partly formed proletariat might come to recognize itself
consciously.

Certainly this turn towards social myth is reflected elsewhere in Joyce's
works. That the crisis and resolution of *Ulysses* is expressed in the language of myth (ibid., 2) echoes the mythic impulse of revolutionary syndicalism. *Ulysses*, like Sorelian social myth, fuses the mythic, especially
moral allegory, with the factual.

This is not unique in Joyce's works and is not confined to a later period
of his writing. According to Ehrlich:

> Previously, in early 1904, Joyce wrote the unpublished first draft ver-
> sion of 'Portrait of the Artist,' using socialist utopian ideology with
> images of man and woman in a future Dublin. It combined in experi-
> mental prose some elements of the socialist manifesto and the aes-
> thetic manifesto, the sexual confession, and the new psychology of
> Bergson. (1997, 87)

This is a crucial connection since it further suggests the link between Sorel,
revolutionary syndicalism and Joyce. Bergson, the vitalistic philosopher,
was a key influence on Sorel who attended Bergson's lectures and incorporated Bergson's notions of *élan vital* as a key feature of his writings on the
mobilizing powers of social myth.[2]

Like the theoretician of revolutionary social myth Sorel, Joyce ascribes an
important role not to a specific class but to the creative strata within struggle,
those who can shape the social myth. "Here the power he ascribes to the artist's Word — to incarnate the millennial State and race — breathes through the

---

2   One might also make note of the importance of ideas Joyce borrowed from Vico
    whose emphasis on corsi and ricorsi in the writing of history greatly influenced Sorel.

mythopoetic, ritualistic diction of his own prose" (Sherry 2004, 13). Joyce's appeal to the artist to ring in the coming revolution takes on the tone and force of a revolutionary manifesto. In the manner of the revolutionary social myth, Joyce's call to the artist invokes the new world gestating in the shell of the old, a new world born of the united social, economic and sexual revolutions. This is expressed most notably in Joyce's famous words from the 1904 draft of *Portrait of the Artist*:

> To those multitudes not yet in the wombs of humanity but surely engenderable there, he would give the word. Man and woman, out of you comes the nation that is to come, the lightening of your masses in travail; the competitive order is employed against itself, the aristocracies are supplanted; and amid the general paralysis of an insane society, the confederate will issues in action (Joyce, 265–266).

This invocation of the artist as heroic herald of a new world is certainly a break with most of anarchist writing, as I have outlined previously. It speaks to Joyce's unique approach and the influence of individualist currents in anarchism. This individualist turn has provided some of the basis for the evidence of those who cite Joyce's supposed turn to authoritarianism. Scholes argues most strenuously that this represents a turn towards the authoritarian in Joyce's work. Certainly there is some basis for taking such a position and raising concerns about possible consequences of such an approach, as the curious path of Sorel himself suggests. In his later years that prophet of working class will exerted through the social myth succumbed to endorsements of both Lenin and Mussolini. Indeed the turn to express social visions in art, especially the privileging of literary authorship found its corollary in the political authoritarianism of Pound and Wyndham Lewis (Sherry 2004, 13).

Another view however suggests that the view of the artist-hero in Joyce has affinities with anti-authoritarian ideas. Dominic Manganiello connects expressions of Joyce's political consciousness with individualist anarchism of the type articulated by the nineteenth-century American anarchist Benjamin Tucker. For Manganiello, this connection with Tucker's anarchism, with which Joyce was familiar and found appealing, sheds light on Joyce's views of the artist as herald of a new world. Brian Caraher explains this perspective as such:

> In place of the encircling and coercive tyrannies of existing social and political institutions, the individualist anarchist as artist employs the resisting power of the clarifying and redeeming word. (Caraher 1999, 175–176).

Manganiello develops this position on political resistance through refer-ence to this passage in the twenty-fourth chapter of *Stephen Hero*: "the art-ist as literary Messiah reconstructs the spectacle of redemption and legitimizes his role of redeemer in his works by affirming that which pre-sumptive States and presumptive Churches negate" (Manganiello 1980, 76).

Joyce's articulation of aesthetic concerns with ideals of individualism and freedom from authoritarianism is also reflected in his attraction to the position offered in that other famous work of idiosyncratic socialism, Oscar Wilde's essay "The Soul of Man under Socialism." Both literary and libertarian socialist affinities rest behind Joyce's decision to become the official translator of Oscar Wilde's classic of libertarian socialism. Accord-ing to Manganiello,

> Joyce probably realized for the first time in Wilde's tract that his demand for absolute freedom to accomplish his aesthetic aims could be made consonant with the political views of Tucker, who stressed respect for individual liberties. (ibid., 220–222)

Significantly the socialist influences on Joyce may have upheld his funda-mental resistance to the political perspective of the authoritarian modern-ists. Joyce gave voice to very personal political and social concerns which were informed by his libertarian understanding of socialism. According to Heyward Ehrlich:

> In his projection of a higher political order, Joyce believed that coura-geous personal acts, such as his elopement with Nora without mar-riage, and his continuing rejection of the church after the birth of their children, required the ideological support of socialist political princi-ples. (Ehrlich 1997, 83)

Socialist principles were not abandoned but expressed in novel ways that in his concern for individual liberty stood opposed to authoritarianism. According to Sherry:

> Pound's glorification of a hieratic priesthood, his esteem for ancient echelons of title and class, locate an authoritarian demeanor alien to Joyce. To that 'aristocracy of the arts' [in Pound] Joyce would oppose 'the confederate will.' The difference leads him, first of all to a socialist politics, ultimately to a dialogic language that orchestrates differences, pluralities, tolerances. (Sherry 2004, 14)

Indeed this language—the language of Joyce's works—is a language of anarchy as political philosophy. Indeed one may see in this a hint of the relation that Todd May and Saul Newman suggest in their work on anar-chy as the first postmodernism.

As Ehrlich (1997, 82) suggests, Joyce's radical social ideals were essential elements in his development as a modernist artist. Throughout his work Joyce explored the possibilities of a new society as well as new visions of the people who might make up that society. Ehrlich notes that in breaking dramatically from the traditions of church, nation and family Joyce "acted not only out of his desire to become a writer but also from a unified set of radical convictions about society, sexuality and art" (ibid.). The personal and social impulses of the "in-between" coincide.

The "in-between" class, including of course many artists, lacking neither the capital nor the social power of a mass proletariat to effect large-scale social change was often left with a pursuit of mythic and heroic forces that might mobilize societal transformation towards their interests. As Ehrlich suggests, Joyce empowers the emerging artist, striving to be free from the dual restraints of class and gender stereotypes, to utter "the word," as the old competitive aristocracies and their "insane society" are replaced by the new general will, the mythic force, of the hopeful and active masses (ibid., 88). Joyce's sexual radicalism is expressed in gender-neutral or androgynous phrasings: "the wombs of humanity" and "man and woman, out of you comes the nation" (ibid.). This is not to subscribe to any class essentialism or structural determinism but rather to try to understand the complexity of subject positions and concerns and their articulation with/in socialist discourse. Joyce gives voice to the hopes and anxieties of a socialism that is largely unrecognized in commentaries on the subject of his politics as well as within commentaries on socialism of the early twentieth century.

Again, Joyce expressed a heterodox socialism drawn not, as for most conventional Marxism, from an understanding of the industrial proletariat and exploitation in labor, but rather from everyday experiences of oppression and struggle in various spheres of life. As Ehrlich suggests:

> When Joyce regarded himself as a socialist or anarchist, he often relied on the political education he received not in the factory or on the farm but rather from his own family as a direct witness of the warfare between his father and mother. (Ehrlich 1997, 82).

In this sense Joyce expresses a sharp recognition of the idea that the personal is also political, a key insight of feminist movements that emerged in the last quarter of the twentieth century.

For Joyce, this understanding that the personal was political set his anarchic socialism against not only capitalist exploitation but against a range of oppressive hierarchies that were more deeply rooted in everyday relations. According to Stanislaus, the basis for Joyce's radicalism was this

fundamental opposition to what he viewed as an ongoing feudalism, associated most directly with the brutal violence directed by their father
against their mother and sisters. "He calls himself a socialist but attaches
himself to no school of socialism. He marks the uprooting of feudal principles" (Joyce 1971, 54). Against feudalism, Joyce offered his visions of modernism as influenced by his complex approach to libertarian socialism.

In an unpublished story, "Silhouettes," the narrator stops in front of a
"row of mean little houses" and witnesses in a window the shadows of a
man and woman "in violent agitation" (Joyce quoted in Ehrlich 1997, 85).
Ehrlich suggests that "Silhouettes" offers "the prototype for the recurring
warfare that rages in Joyce's early fiction between the drunken, brutal
father and the young children protected by their mother" (ibid., 86). This
battle is depicted in several of the stories in *Dubliners*, most notably in
"Counterparts" and "Eveline," and to a lesser degree in "A Little Cloud"
and "Araby."

This draws attention to a crucial complexity in Joyce's approach to
socialism. Indeed it calls to mind the long-overlooked concerns of another
idiosyncratic socialist, and proto-anarchist, Charles Fourier and his utopian writings on liberating the passions, rather than any of the mainstream
versions of socialism in Joyce's time. According to Ehrlich:

> Joyce's socialism gave him a way of cutting the three ties to church,
> nation, and family: the socialists were commonly seen as Rome's
> prime enemy; they were international, not national, in scope; and their
> tradition of utopianism had offered ample alternate models to bour-
> geois family life. (ibid.)

All of this occurs in a context in which the specter of a sexual revolution in
Ireland appeared more dangerous even than a political revolution. Joyce's
writings on the ill treatment of women, which Brown (1985) identifies as
feminist, are informed by his socialism and sexual liberalism. Such domestic concerns were central for the outlook of anarchists during Joyce's era.
Indeed anarchist concerns with such everyday oppressions, as distinct
from the daily exploitation experienced in the workplace, marked their
analysis as unique with respect to much of the socialist movement.

If Cixous is mistaken in viewing Joyce as politically disengaged, she is
correct in identifying his conscience as one of exile and heresy. In his *Letters*,
Joyce describes his relation to the established social order as that of a vagabond. As Ehrlich notes: "For Joyce to be a 'vagabond' was to build a base of
radical philosophical and social principles for future artistic activity" (1997,
83). His exile and heresy suggest the rootlessness of the déclassé, characteristic for many artists. In more contemporary language he evokes conditions
of nomadology or exile as contestatory against the power of states.

> Joyce articulated a position of antibourgeois and antiauthoritarian
> resistance, but he located the source and focus of such political con-
> sciousness not in an international collective of workers but in an
> empowering individualism that he personally regarded as his own 're-
> deemer' — the term he uses in the sixteenth chapter of the discarded
> and fragmentary text of *Stephen Hero*. (Caraher 1999, 176)

In a brief sketch written for his brother Stanislaus, Joyce provided a picture of the political and personal ideals that marked his work.

> [Scene: drafty little stone-flagged room, chest of drawers to left, on
> which are the remains of lunch, in the centre, a small table on which are
> *writing materials* (He never forgot them) and a saltcellar: in the back-
> ground, small-sized bed. A young man with snivelling nose sits at the
> little table: on the bed sit a madonna and a plaintive infant. It is a Janu-
> ary day.] Title of above: *The Anarchist*. (1966, 206, quoted in Ehrlich
> 1997, 84)

Ehrlich suggests that this sketch "affirms Joyce's views of the nobility of
poverty, art, exile, sexual freedom, religious nonconformity, and social
and political dissent" (ibid.).

   In the end one might readily agree with James Fairhall's conclusion: "The
critic trying to identify Joyce with any particular discourse faces an impossible task, since no one discourse is privileged or indeed has any meaning
except in dialogue with other discourses" (Fairhall 1993, 60). The discussion
in this chapter invites some other discourses, ones that have been
marginalized or excluded, into that dialogue. These discourses, illustrating
the complex character of Joyce's socialism, show, as Caraher suggests, that
"readers of Joyce's work and life can disclose factual divergences and contrasting evidence that complicate an easy overlay of any single typology or
semiotic code" (1999, 176). These notes on the idiosyncratic socialism of
Joyce — his anarchism — may allow for a more complex understanding of
Joyce's politics and artistic interests than that suggested by theses of Joyce's
move from internationalism to authoritarianism.

Chapter Six

Beyond socialist realism

Anarchism and glocal concerns in the writings of Wole Soyinka

The poetry of African poets over the last several decades asserts a fierceness, passion, originality and vitality that is lacking from much of recent western poetry (Moore, 1998). Indeed, African poets are presenting some of the most compelling and exciting poetry in the world. The lack of broad discussion of and attention to African poetry is surprising given both the traditional significance of poetry in many African cultures and the creative power of recent African poets. The poems (of struggle) affirm another Africa, beyond the gloom and sorrow presented as the only face of Africa in the western press. An appreciation and understanding of African poetry is essential in the current context where many are turning to cultural expressions opposed to the processes and effects of capitalist globalization.

> Not only the familiar ones of poverty and oppression, but those newly imposed by the IMF, with its insistence on cuts in health and education services, which mortgage the future as well as the present. And all this to the background of an international community that veers between blundering interference and cynical indifference; between using helicopter gunships to hunt down a single man and turning its back on genocide. (ibid., xxiv)

In this poetry is a refusal to succumb, to let go of fundamental values. In the works of certain contemporary African poets one finds challenging perspectives within revolutionary thought that go beyond the categories and visions of much art or revolutionary theory. These poets raise alternatives based on the practices, values and ideas of indigenous forms of social organization which have been de-valued by some variants of socialism.

Listening to voices that express viable African alternatives offers various benefits, "not the least of which is the opportunity it offers black Africa to become a source of usable ideas, rather than merely a consumer of them" (Owomoyela 1991, 36). This is as important as ever in the age of globalization as the circulation of social struggles and social visions is vibrantly and vitally expressed in processes of engagement that will shape the future of life on the planet. In these poems one can catch glimpses of organizing for self-determination and the undermining of oppressive systems. These glimpses offer responses to the pressing problems and challenges facing people around the globe. African poets like Wole Soyinka strive to see and understand their postcolonial (or neocolonial) worlds differently in order to resist, to fight back. Their works also offer new insights for others trying to fight back. At the same time these poets manage to avoid the risks some poets face of succumbing to rhetorical commonplaces as they struggle to put forward a political vision. There is no confusion of propaganda with art or substitution of propaganda for art. These poets do not compromise or sacrifice their artistry to make a political point.

Beyond socialist realism: socialism by tendency and glocal concerns

According to contemporary anarchist commentator Ashanti Alston (2003, online), the contemporary works of African poets ask us "to accept the validity of a non-western perspective and way of making sense of life." In doing so, the works of African poets offer an important opportunity for global activists to move beyond the confines of Eurocentric and authoritarian political theories as well as providing a point of departure for anti-authoritarian activists to develop broadened insights into community-based resistance to the predations of neo-liberal capitalist globalization.

This will not necessarily be an easy task. As Alston notes:

> This may prove difficult for Marxists, anarcho-communists, and syndicalists who have learned to see the world only through the lens of science, reason and objectivity, with 'the worker' as the epicenter of change. (ibid.)

Commentators and critics working from a Soviet socialist realist perspective have offered harsh evaluations of the sociopolitical visions of contemporary African poets.

This is not a prejudice that is confined to western critics. Owomoyela (1991, 25) suggests that African leftist critics are "scrupulously faithful to non-African models of conceptualization and terminology" and because of their preference for European models "might more appropriately be designated as Euro-Marxists." Significant commentaries such as Olafioye's *Politics in African Poetry* have implied that African poetry is inferior to western poetry because African poets are too concerned with national issues while western poets speak to global issues. Within such perspectives, western cultures and discourses are held as universal while African alternatives are "aggressively derided" (ibid., 29). This criticism is entirely misguided, however, as it sidesteps the avoidance of politics that characterizes most western poetry. Even more it overlooks the important voices of African poets who have spoken out against such global issues as apartheid and neo-liberal adjustment. Ngara (1990) for example is impatient with Soyinka's nativism for its supposed failure to lead to "ideologically correct" visions of Africa's future. For Ngara (ibid., 200), poets like Soyinka are inadequately devoted to "new and progressive forms of social consciousness." Unfortunately, this assessment by Ngara is based on the "revelations of Marxism" (ibid., 197).

This is perhaps not surprising given the significance of Marxism in certain phases of African poetry. Ojaide (1995, 18) notes that by the 1970s Marxist-inspired "socialism had a firm grip on the minds of young African intellectuals." Into the 1980s many writers (Ugah, Osundare, Ngugi) identified as socialists. Of course this was typically a statist version of socialism rooted in alliances shown by Stalinist regimes in the USSR and China with emergent or young states in Africa such as Angola and Mozambique. This formed a pole of attraction against the exploitative interests of Western capitalism. As Ojaide suggests: "The workers and the common people sought the assistance of socialist countries. It was the Eastern bloc that cared for the have-nots, because their workers ruled and knew the problems of the working class and the disadvantaged" (ibid., 18). Ojaide recalls: "Socialism entered African literature to reinforce the tradition itself and especially the activist role of the verbal artist" (ibid.). Much criticism has approached African poetry in terms of supposed universals. Marxist commentators have focused especially on presumed universals such as class. Others, arguing against Marxist interpretations have preferred to speak in terms of ethnicity or kinship. I do not intend to dismiss or denigrate either of these approaches. Instead I prefer to give attention to the possibilities of alternative visions and approaches.

Both the sociopolitical concerns and the visions of future social relations have undergone tremendous development in the post-socialist era of neo-liberal capitalist globalism. Recent social and artistic movements emerging through opposition to capitalist globalization have emphasized the convergence of local and global concerns, what some have termed "glocalization" or "glocality." From this perspective attention is given to locally rooted experiences, and especially experiences of struggle and resistance, that have global implications or address global concerns. These are not universalist or universalizing discourses which seek to present themselves as world historical or epoch-making. These glocal themes include pressing concerns for the natural environment and local communities as well as libertarian or anarchist visions of social regeneration along radically democratic lines beyond the authoritarianism of the state, including Marxist states. These themes express local visions and values derived from local experiences rather than the models of imported systems of thought. These visions and values suggest the continuation of radicalism within African poetry but in forms that are not easily categorized within the framework of Marxist socialism. As Ojaide (1995, 18) has proclaimed: "I myself was socialist in tendency but rejected being an ideologue." This is a key distinction.

> There are indications that despite the demise of communism in Eastern Europe, the flowering of multi-party politics in Africa, and the gradual dismantling of apartheid in South Africa, African poetry will continue to be radical. This is because of the debt burden created by the IMF and the World Bank and the worsening socio-economic plight of African countries. Thus, even though the ideological point has been blunted in international politics, there will still be strident calls for the amelioration of the plight of the abused masses. Poets will continue to portray the bleak socio-economic landscape with negative and ugly images and dream of light at the end of the tunnel. (ibid., 17)

Focus on socialism by tendency, drawn from glocal experiences and cultures, moves discussion of African literature beyond dualistic conceptualizations which posit a choice between socialist realism or African realism (Owomoyela 1991). At the same time it allows for proper recognition of emerging social(ist) visions in a post-Soviet age.

It offers some assistance in evaluating the political vision in Soyinka's writing, for example, by refusing to view as reactionary or anti-socialist his attention to Yoruba myths and traditions. It also avoids the contempt for Soyinka's work by others who view it as an appropriation of African culture within a western framework. Again, the view presented here allows a new space for understanding beyond ideological dualisms.

If western critics and commentators have overlooked African poetry, western activists have also failed to engage with African political expressions. This is perhaps especially true for anarchists. Major histories of anarchism as well as collections of anarchist writers have almost entirely excluded any mention of anarchist or libertarian visions that have emerged within Africa. Still some anarchists have begun to develop a respect for the insights of the indigenous thinkers and localist approaches to questions of knowledge beyond the limits of Western social science. As anarchist philosopher Paul Feyerabend has noted, it is now necessary

> to reexamine our attitude towards myth, religion, magic, witchcraft and towards all those ideas which rationalists would like to see forever removed from the surface of the earth (without so much as having looked at them—a typical taboo reaction). (Feyerabend 1975, online)

Of course, while these intentions and concerns are well-taken, one must avoid replicating Eurocentric dualisms in contrasting western rationality with supposed African emotionalism. This is a mistake that Wole Soyinka both identifies and attempts to overcome. The poems belong simultaneously to the history of western poetry and the worlds of colonial and postcolonial African writing.

The organic anarchism of Wole Soyinka

While most known for his dramatic works, Wole Soyinka's wide ranging works include poetry, literary and cultural criticism, *Myth, Literature and the African World*; and political commentary, *The Open Sore of a Continent*. It was in recognition of the power of these diverse writings that Wole Soyinka was named the first African to win the Nobel Prize for Literature in 1986.

It is well known that Soyinka drew inspiration from the works of Franz Fanon, Amilcar Cabral, Kwame Nkrumah and Julius Nyerere. It is perhaps less well known that Soyinka also engaged with the works of such anarchist or libertarian thinkers as Pierre-Joseph Proudhon, Tolstoy and Albert Camus (Stratton, 1988). Along with these influences Soyinka's philosophical roots are deeply grounded in Yoruban culture and mythology.

It is in the organic mix of Yoruban and western understandings of African mythology that Soyinka locates an anarchist presence (Alston 2003). His analysis of the postcolonial disappointments and reversals of African political dynamics and his call for an "organic revolution" that derives its power and authenticity from Yoruban cultural mythology has made his work both unique and controversial (ibid.). In his poems as much as his other works Soyinka has dissected the ongoing abuses of power that colonialism has fostered in generations of political leadership and state functionaries. This has placed Soyinka the poet alongside political commentators like Fanon and Nkrumah in highlighting the class contradictions and other impediments of nationalism and neocolonialism. This is a critical vision that Soyinka has maintained for four decades as a citizen-rebel artist (ibid.).

Walunywa (1997) suggests that Soyinka's work poses the question whether the ritual drama in "endogenous society" might provide means for anarchic regeneration, recuperation and a praxis of the "creative-destructive principle" in contemporary life. Walunywa (1997) notes the recurrent anarchist themes that run through Soyinka's work in the representation and play with Yoruban myth and ritual drama. Soyinka's work provides a glimpse of anarchism that is based in African reality and, notably, in ritual or tragic drama. Indeed, his anarchism speaks of and through the ritual drama of endogenous society (Alston, 2003).

In his study of Soyinka's work, Walunywa (1997, 21) argues that Soyinka has introduced a specific form of anarchism in African intellectual discourse. The anarchism that Walunywa identifies in Soyinka's writings is defined as the desire on the part of the individual concerned to deconstruct the social, economic and political institutions which reflect the values of "modern civilization" as conceptualized through the prevailing ideologies in order to pave the way for the recuperation of "primordial culture" as conceptualized through the "cosmologies" of "endogenous societies." (ibid.)

This anarchism shares with other varieties of anarchism

> the consistent resistance — the desire to break free of — all forces, irrespective of whether they originate from 'the Left' or from 'the Right,' that seek to confine either the individual or the community within any established social, economic, or political constitutional barricade. (ibid., 75)

The endogenous anarchism expressed by Soyinka refers to specific mythological or symbolic practices that preceded and in various ways survived the imposition of European colonialist modernity and remain part of cultures that continue their resistance to neocolonialism partly through their myths and rituals (Alston 2003). These are the cultural expressions of indigenous societies.

> They are endogenous reenactments of the unity, contradiction and struggle of existence; ritual archetypal reenactments found the world over that highlight and 'myth poeticize' such dramatic themes as death and rebirth, disintegration and recuperation, destruction and creation, suffering and compassion, fragmentation and re-assemblage, and fallibility and remediation. (ibid.)

These traditions carry mechanisms for ongoing resistance, revision, regeneration and revolution (ibid.). According to Walunywa (1997, 22):

> the primary function upon which endogenous society is developed — 'the ritual archetype' — is believed to be 'revolutionary' in terms of the freedom it affords the individual and the community because it is thought to provide the medium through which the individual and the community in question maintain an intimate relationship with primordial culture and its liberating forces (and consequently exist in a diametrical opposition with modern culture and its alienating forces) without completely relinquishing their respective sense of selfhood and community.

Walunywa argues that Soyinka brings the anarchic, communal character of ritual dramas to center stage through his literary works as well as his commentaries on politics and postcolonial revolutions. Notably, Soyinka, found a personal affinity as a youngster with the god Ogun and it is Ogun that he develops as an archetypal anarchist (ibid.). Ogun initiated the return of divinity to humanity. For Soyinka, the transition from confinement and oppression to liberatory existence is a crucial principle. In Soyinka's work Ogun is the principal "transit conductor" (Alston 2003). As Soyinka (1976, 30) suggests: "Ogun is the embodiment of challenge, the Promethean instinct in man, constantly at the service of society for its full self-realization." In Soyinka's work the character of Ogun is recreated in such a way that it "can be most useful in the context of Africa's contemporary post-colonial, neo-liberal wreckage" (Alston 2003).

Soyinka places Ogun at the center of Yoruban metaphysics. Indeed, this "Ogunian anarchism is the theme that constantly expresses itself throughout Soyinka's art, life and revolutionary vision" (ibid.).

> He is the individualist anarchist, the iron worker, the reluctant leader, or Nietzsche's Superman, expressing the indomitable will to power (according to Soyinka) in the service of community. He is the only god willing to make the transition through the abyss, through the chaos, to prepare the way for the others in their quest to reunify with humanity. In making the transition, he is also willing to be torn asunder, so that in re-assemblage he might help bring about communal change. (ibid.)

The activities of Ogun assert the principle of destruction and creativity regularly invoked by anarchists such as Bakunin. This is not necessarily a pleasant journey but in it one might find the forces upon which creativity and regeneration might be realized. This transition, in which the individual working for the community lets go of itself within the context of the ritual, "implies being torn asunder from all those alienating forces and ideological influences, individually and collectively internalized, that has kept one stuck in a restricted state" (ibid.).

According to Osundare (1994, 81), in Soyinka's work the Atunda/ Atooda paradigm, in which the slave Atunda shatters the god Orisanla to fragments with a boulder, also plays a key part. The paradigm presents the basis for a "supra-segmental ontology" of "multiplicity without chaos" as accidental fissures resolve themselves "into a plural unity." The Atunda paradigm, and Soyinka's invocation of it, offers a "fascinating mix of creative rebelliousness and rebellious creativeness" (ibid.). With the smashing of an absolutist hegemony comes a creative plurality.

> Union they had known until the Boulder
> Rolling down the Hill of the Beginning
> Shred the kernel to a million lights.
> A traitor's heart rejoiced, the god's own slave
> Dirt-covered from the deed. (Soyinka 1967, 68)

From the destructive act comes an act of creation.

> Man's passage, pre-ordained, self-ordered winds
> In reconstruction. (Piecemeal was *their* deft
> Re-birth). (ibid., 69)

In the words of Osundare, like Ogun, "Atunda creates new orders by destroying the old Order, engineers a polyphony of accents from one invariate Voice" (Osundare 1994, 84). As the anarchist Bakunin famously proclaimed: "The urge for destruction is a creative passion also." So it is with Ogun and Atunda. In both, "the act of creation is locked in dialectical combat with the act of destruction" (ibid.).

Again, like Atunda, the anarchist is the "lone figure" who through an "assertive act" brings about epochal transformations (Soyinka 1967, 16; 18). The anarchist is the stray electron celebrated by Soyinka in *Idanre*.

> ... may we celebrate the stray electron, defiant
> Of patterns, celebrate the splitting of the gods
> Canonisation of the strong hand of a slave who set
> The rock in revolution ... (ibid., 82)

As in anarchist suggestions that the means and ends of struggle are interconnected, in the figure of Atunda "a mythic fusion occurs of act and actor, process and person" (Osundare 1994, 82).

Take note of the similarity between Marx's invocation that each class produces its own gravediggers in relation to the suggestion in Osundare's discussion of the Atunda/Atooda paradigm in Soyinka's work:

> In a way, every Orisanla needs an Atunda, or more appropriately, every Orisanla creates his own Atunda, the chink in an elaborate, overdetermined armour, facilitator of a revolution made inevitable by a crass, obvious hegemony. (ibid., 83)

Indeed the call to direct action moves Soyinka's telling away from the realm of saints, despite his reference in *Idanre*, to "Saint Atunda, First Revolutionary" (Soyinka 1967, 83). In *A Shuttle in the Crypt*, Soyinka expresses impatience with the evolutionary contemplation of the saint.

> No saint—are saints not moved beyond
> Event, their passive valour turned to time's
> Slow unfolding? (Soyinka 1972, 21)

In his reference to Hamlet, "the prince of doubts" in *A Shuttle in the Crypt*, Soyinka offers a symbol

> for those dithering, prevaricating, procrastinating 'intellectuals' of the Ivory Tower ... ever ready to intellectualise and justify rank manifestations of the state's disease ... These are the ghost-writers, special advisers, and hungry consultants to depraved governments, spongers on a nation's wealth—and will—more of madmen than specialists. (Osundare 1994, 89)

Instead of paralyzing contemplation, he calls for immediate and decisive direct action.

> A time of evil cries
> Renunciation of the saintly vision
> Summons instant hands of truth to tear
> All painted masks. (Soyinka 1972, 21)

Beyond criticizing corrupt or despotic leaders there is growing analysis and criticism of national middle classes of which many poets themselves are a part. This is often expressed in criticisms of the academic communities, again home to many poets, where rhetorical opposition is sometimes not matched by action.

In "My Tongue Does Not Marry Slogans" Soyinka offers a sharp rebuke of such paper tiger leftist academics:

> Midnight missed you at the barricades
> But found you snoring sweetly in your mistress's
> Arms, secured by campus walls, manned
> Day and night by 'wage slave proletarians.' (Soyinka 1988)

The poem "Ujamaa" from *A Shuttle in the Crypt* is dedicated to Julius Nyerere, a figure of much interest for libertarian socialists. In the poem, Soyinka offers a powerful vision of the communal solidarity of workers and the land that sustains them.

> Sweat is leaven for the earth
> Not driven homage to a fortressed god.
> Your black earth hands unchain
> Hope from death messengers. (Soyinka 1972, 80)

In the manner of radical ecologists and green anarchists, nature, rather than an adversary to be overcome through Promethean development, is the sustainer of communities. At the same time, labor must be self-determined, not exploited as "homage to a fortressed god," even a proletarian one. Soyinka affirms the connection between nature and community, against even Marxist progressivism:

> Bread of the earth, by the earth
> For the earth. Earth is all people. (ibid.)

Soyinka's poems stand as shining examples of the work of the glocal poet, rooted in local experiences but speaking across boundaries. As Osundare (1994, 93) suggests:

> Soyinka is a poet of unlimited latitude, a free-ranging, though stubbornly rooted spirit for whom the entire world is a legitimate constituency. His fame stirs the lips of the Four Winds, but his charity always begins at home.

Marxist socialist critics have assailed Soyinka for not being an explicit socialist (see Hunt 1985). Geoffrey Hunt has derided Soyinka's interest/focus on Yoruban history as romantic escapism.

On the other hand, Owomoyela (1991, 22) suggests that Soyinka "has been a rather attractive target for the leftists because, even though he epitomizes the maturity of African literature, he does not satisfy the ideological expectations of the Marxists." Balogun (1988) has argued that Marxist critics of Soyinka, who accuse him of not being a socialist, have misread his works. Balogun suggests that while Soyinka has not identified himself explicitly as a socialist, his works do espouse socialism. A focus on the libertarian or anarchist impulses of Soyinka's work may help to address and clear up some of the debates over Soyinka's relation to socialism. Looking at Soyinka's work in relation to anarchistic currents situates it within a broader socialist stream, notably a libertarian and anti-statist socialism. His is a socialism by tendency.

Conclusion

It has long been noted that social, political and economic histories have greatly impacted the development of writing on the continent (see Jahn 1961; Mutiso 1974; Ojaide 1995). During the early independence period one commentator noted that major global concerns are expressed in African poetry while interpreting them through "the peculiarly African experience that is superimposed on that of the common denominator of world concerns" (Mphalele 1967, 12). Colonialism and independence and its many convulsions and neocolonialism provide a certain commonality for African poets. These forces, which are profoundly global, also provide a deep resonance with people engaged in struggle against oppression and exploitation in other parts of the globe. This resonance is especially meaningful in the current age of neo-liberal capitalist globalization as movements in defense of community emerge on every continent to assert that "another world is possible." The poems form a vibrant document of the political developments of people in struggle. At the same time their appeal extends well beyond the conditions of their emergence.

Ojaide suggests that the "contemporary African writer has become a warrior of sorts, ever devising new strategies to deflect bullets from himself and still knock down the enemy" (1995, 18). In his view:

> Poetry, indeed all African literature, has become the guidebook for achieving certain goals to benefit the common people. The poet has become primarily an activist. (ibid.)

Yet the activism and activist concerns of the contemporary poets may be almost unrecognizable to earlier generations of political poets, artists and commentators.

> At this stage I feel that condemnation and lamentation are not enough for the African. I believe that commemoration of all that is good in the past and is still viable but ignored in the present should inspire hope. We need not write dirges for the living. For me there is hope, and that should be the common pursuit of African writers. We should be build-

ers. Our vision should be such that it will raise us from the current low
state to high hopes of what we can be. (ibid., 21)

Soyinka puts forward visions of socioeconomic resistance and transformation but without necessarily being mass-oriented or ideologically
informed in the manner of traditional left poets. At the same time his
poetry takes up the plight of the poor, dispossessed, workers and peasants. His works also show a deep concern for the land and the ecological
depredations wrought by imperialist development.

Ojaide (1995, 4) notes that poetry in Africa is "currently enjoying an
unprecedented creative outburst and popularity." Many new writers have
been encouraged by the continent's burgeoning poetry workshops. Poetry
books are receiving a wider readership and larger audiences attend reading sessions. All of this has contributed to a certain popularization of a
medium once considered to be elitist, intellectual and obscure (ibid.). At
the same time the cost of books has become prohibitive in many areas in
Africa which hampers publication. After the economic restructuring experienced by many multinational publishers beginning in the 1980s, major
publishing houses came to publish little African poetry. Works by new
poets are often difficult to come by due to the difficulties facing small publishers. Local publishers are constrained by economic conditions and have
limited their publications of poetry. Even presses in North America and
Britain that publish African poets cannot adequately expose emerging
poets (ibid.). Thus there are some obstacles that may impede the circulation of African poetry to other parts of the globe where they might be taken
up by activists. Hopefully the present work can at least provide an opening for global, or rather, glocal readers to begin an engagement with African poets.

Chapter Seven

Novel utopias

Feminism and anarchism in the works of Ursula K. LeGuin

As noted previously, perhaps the most widespread popular image of anarchism is the menacing figure of the black trenchcoat-wearing, bearded man who moves in the shadows holding a bomb. He is the man of action and intrigue. Lyman Tower Sargent (1983) suggests that it would be more appropriate for women to be the symbol of anarchism, given not only the actual support for anarchism by women historically, but also the important convergences between anarchism and feminism in theory and in practice.

In the last decades of the twentieth century, many women writers in particular have expressed anarchist visions within a range of utopian writings, notably in the form of science fiction novels and stories. These writers, influenced by the movements and politics of the 1960s and 1970s, especially feminism, environmentalism, anti-war, and global justice, have brought anarchist and feminist perspectives together in their creative imaging of social relations and social organization.

Anarchists have used science fiction narratives to describe social life organized along anarchist lines. Their work presents anarchist utopias but offers key clues as to how such worlds might be realized—how they might play out in reality. As such they are often better understood as heterotopian. Science fiction provides a venue for critical works, but has been dismissed until recently. In the words of Ursula K. LeGuin:

> Science fiction and fantasy slip under the wire a lot, you know? People just aren't looking for radical thought in a field the respectable critics define as escapist drivel. Some of it is escapist all right, but what it's

escaping is the drivel of popular fiction and most TV and movies. (Quoted in Killjoy 2009, 11).

As Emma Goldman has argued even romantic works can provide venues for subversion.

Ursula K. LeGuin is one of several recent authors who actively and openly engage with anarchist theory and practice. LeGuin's work, like that of many other feminist writers of the 1960s and 1970s, reflects important shifts in anarchist thought during that period. Particularly it reflects the growing importance of non-economic, or supra-class, issues (or at least the intersection of economic and non-economic issues) and issues of identity within anarchist politics.

Ursula K. LeGuin

Ursula K. LeGuin represents one of the most powerful feminist voices in science fiction. For decades her work has offered thoughtful explorations of the challenges and promise of anti-authoritarian and feminist social relations. LeGuin impacted the male dominated world of science fiction writing in the late 1960s and early 1970s. She offered strong women characters and, unlike most science fiction writers, presented people of color as heroes.

Perhaps more than most writers influenced by anarchism, Ursula K. LeGuin openly and consciously presents anarchist ideas, debates, and perspectives in her fiction. Among the generation of feminist fiction writers to emerge in the 1960s and 1970s, LeGuin has most explicitly presented, and continues to present, her visions as anarchist in influence and intent. Her most famous anarchist work is also her most well known work, *The Dispossessed*. Her work *The Left Hand of Darkness* explores issues of gender and the transgression of gender categories as a central aspect of human personal and social liberation.

LeGuin is also keen in pointing out anarchist concerns for ecology. Any anarchist future must be one that moves beyond human domination of nature. Part of achieving free, ecological societies is a renewal of respect for women's labor and women's wisdom and knowledge. Control of their own labor by women, and the broader choices that allows, emerge as key themes.

Even her less explicitly anarchist works reflect on the constructed and contested basis of social relations and the importance of mutual aid within social life. At the same time LeGuin is always realistic and honest in illustrating the difficulties facing attempts to realize anarchist social relations.

The Dispossessed

Her most appreciated and influential work, *The Dispossessed*, is a detailed exploration of the promise and problems of attempts to develop an anarchist alternative society. *The Dispossessed* is unique in that it focuses, often starkly, on difficulties facing utopian social relations as they develop over time. Rather than a fixed society, the utopian world, in this case the unambiguously named "Annares," is faced with the necessity of ongoing change—sometimes undesired change. Indeed, the reader is struck by the emphasis LeGuin places on the foibles and failings of Annares and its sometimes frustrated inhabitants. *The Dispossessed* is subtitled *An Ambiguous Utopia*. As Tower Sargent suggests, rather than a perfect world of perfect people, Annares represents "a harsh, cruel, unforgiving world peopled by real human beings with all their faults" (1983, 10). Yet even imperfect people can struggle to improve their imperfect utopia.

Annares is a stateless society. This does not mean that it is ungoverned or uncoordinated or unorganized. In the words of the protagonist Shevek:

> The network of administration and management is called PDC, Production and Distribution Coordination. They are a coordinating system for all syndicates, federatives, and individuals that do productive work. They do not govern persons; they administer production. They have no authority either to support me or to prevent me. They can only tell us the public opinion of us—where we stand in the social conscience. (LeGuin 1974, 67)

Key to the anarchist structure of Annares is decentralization and dispersion of power. In Annares:

> Decentralization had been an essential element in Odo's plans for the society she did not live to see founded. She had no intention to de-urbanize civilization. Though she suggested that the natural limit to the size of a community lay in its dependence on its own immediate region for essential food and power, she intended that all communities be connected by communication and transportation networks, so that

> goods and ideas could get where they were wanted, and the adminis-
> tration of things might work with speed and ease, and no community
> should be set off from change and interchange. But the network was
> not to run from the top down. (ibid., 83–84)

Thus, LeGuin brings to life key aspects of recent anarchist thought. These
include bioregionalism, horizontalism, and federation. Bioregionalism
speaks to approaches in environmentalism, inspired by anarchism, that
stress local production and social organization according to natural ecosys-
tems rather than according to false nation state boundaries or international
trade and transportation. Horizontal federation refers to the interconnec-
tedness of communities for intercourse and exchange — but on the basis of
equality and mutuality rather than the superiority or rule of one community
over another.

If decentralization characterizes political organization in Annares, the
economic life of the community is based on free cooperation. Each person
voluntarily gives a day of community labor for every ten days or decad
(Tower Sargent 1983, 12). This is labor directed toward personal and community needs, or "use values" in Marxist terms, rather than toward
exchange value or profit. The key issue is not economic profitability but
personal and social justice. The structure of work is described as follows:

> Most Annarresti worked five to ten hours a day, with two to four days
> off for each decad. Details of regularity, punctuality, which days off,
> and so on were worked out between the individual and his work crew
> or gang or syndicate or coordinating federative, on whichever level
> cooperation and efficiency could be achieved. (LeGuin 1974, 164).

Efficiency is understood differently than within a capitalist context based
on the exploitation and appropriation of collective labor for private gain
(of capital). No one can be forced to take even difficult labor and no one is
coerced to take a job they do not wish to do on the basis that they need to
earn a living, as is the case in capitalist societies.

Goods are freely available at community depositories and safeguards
against abuse are provided by informal social controls, particularly public
opinion, and internally adopted norms and values. Education, as anarchists have long advocated, is geared toward social needs. At the same
time, specific talents of individuals are also nurtured and encouraged.

The anarchism of *The Dispossessed* is developed by LeGuin in a later
novel *The Eye of the Heron* (1980). In this story the focus is on non-violence
and themes of exile or escape within the context of libertarian politics. *The
Eye of the Heron* details the conflict between an authoritarian, patriarchal
dystopia The City and dwellers of its Shanty Town. The City was founded

by men who had been exiled from earth to work on a penal colony on a distant planet. The Shanty Town was composed of pacifists who were also exiled to the planet at a later date. The pacifists work as artisans and come to run the economy of the planet, without exploiting either their own members or the members of The City. It is something of a petit bourgeois utopia.

Again, for LeGuin, issues of gender and sexual equality are inseparable from issues of liberty and freedom. Gender and sexual equality are key aspects of anarchist social relations. Women are the property of men in The City and are treated as commodities. Members of The Shanty Town, the Shantish, have developed an anarchic, egalitarian society. Seeking to liberate themselves completely from The City, they exile themselves to a new home in an uninhabited part of the planet.

At the same time LeGuin is clear sighted and honest about the possible limits of close knit, cooperatively run societies. Namely, she warns of the dangers of public opinion. Rather than direct coercion there is the threat of coercive public opinion, the pain of nosiness and rumor. The greater danger of rule by public opinion is conformism and the appearance of voluntarism that can mask dissatisfaction or cover up the gradual erosion of personal or social freedoms. As Shevek complains: "'We've let cooperation become obedience'" (LeGuin 1974, 146). In Annares, difference can become the basis for social difficulty. Those who are particularly creative risk reproach through the popular admonition: "Don't egoize!" Even more, public opinion can be manipulated by those with opportunistic intentions who occupy specific roles in society (Tower Sargent 1983, 11).

The Left Hand of Darkness

LeGuin's work stresses that true freedom is only possible in the context of equality between men and women (and other possible genders). For this equality to be achieved, men will have to undertake important changes. Perhaps the greatest achievement of Annares is expressed in the matters of sexual and gender equality. Even sexual activity is understood as a mutually shared activity. Describing the mutual character of sex in Annares: "It meant something two people did, not something one person did or had" (LeGuin 1974, 47).

LeGuin pursues issues of sexual identities and the intersections of sexuality and social relations perhaps most forcefully in her earlier novel *The Left Hand of Darkness* (1969). *The Left Hand of Darkness* is set on the planet Gethen and examines life in two societies on the planet. Gethenians are hermaphrodites whose regular identities are based on mixed sexuality (woman/man, man/woman) when they are not in their sexually active cycles (Tower Sargent 1983, 14). The sexual cycle occurs over twenty-eight days and only during the period of sexual activity, the period they call *kemmer*, do Gethenians adopt male or female characteristics. Notably, the sex role is only established in each *kemmer* period in interaction with another person (ibid.). Neither male nor female roles are predominant and the outcome of adopted roles is a result of a specific relationship. Sex takes on a position of reduced importance compared with, say, modernist human societies, where people are permanently in a state of *kemmer* (ibid.). The norm of their society is asexuality. *Kemmer* is only a part of a larger cycle. Even more, *kemmer* is not always played in pairs. Indeed it is often the case that "groups may form and intercourse take place promiscuously" (LeGuin 1969, 91). At the same time, some choose a monogamous relationship or *vowing kemmering*. The key emphasis is upon difference and choice. Participants are free to pursue, in conditions of mutuality, the sexual relations and practices that they prefer. None are ranked above others and none are viewed as preferred. Similarly, no consensual relations are degraded or demonized, as in the religiously influenced moral economies of even liberal democracies. As the Ekumenical investigator puts it:

> When you meet a Gethenian you cannot and must not do what a bisexual naturally does, which is to cast him in the role of Man or Woman, while adopting towards him a corresponding role dependent on your expectations of the patterned or possible interactions between persons of the opposite sex. Our entire pattern of socio-sexual interaction is non-existent here. They cannot play the game. They do not see one another as men or women. This is almost impossible for our imagination to accept. What is the first question we ask about a newborn baby?
>
> Yet you cannot think of a Gethenian as 'it.' ...
> One is respected and judged only as a human being. It is an appalling experience. (ibid., 94–95)

Androgyny becomes a requirement for not only women's liberation, but for human liberation. It reflects a social condition in which roles and ways of being can be chosen freely rather than imposed arbitrarily or coerced. For LeGuin, androgyny becomes a mechanism for thinking about or revealing essential characteristics free from the constraints of gender roles.

In her words, she "eliminated gender to find out what was left" (1969, 163).

Parker Rhodes notes the power of the androgyne as a durable human archetype in both eastern and western cultures. From ancient to modern times the figure of the androgyne has held a fascination for human culture. Various cultural mythologies hold that at creation the human was an androgyne—a sexually undifferentiated being (Parker Rhodes 1983, 110). Indeed the end of primordial or mythic time, and the onset of the social, is marked by the splitting of the androgyne (ibid.). One finds famous discussions of the androgyne in works such as Plato's *Symposium* and "Genesis" as well as Jung and de Beauvoir.

Social conditioning confines human potentialities and activities within gender roles and categories (ibid., 111). LeGuin outlines the utopian promise of androgyny:

> Anyone can turn his hand to anything. This sounds very simple, but its psychological effects are incalculable. The fact that everyone between seventeen and thirty-five or so is liable to be (as Nim put it) 'tied down to childbearing,' implies that no one is quite so thoroughly 'tied down' here as women, elsewhere, are likely to be—psychologically or physically. Burden and privilege are shared out pretty equally; everybody has the same risk to run or choice to make. Therefore nobody here is quite so free as a free male anywhere else. (LeGuin 1969, 93)

This means that the 'freedom' of males under patriarchal societies—to rape, to war, to exploitation—are absent. As LeGuin relates, activities are undertaken only with consent and mutual invitation (ibid.).

In a language that prefigures recent post-structuralist theorizing in the works of Derrida and Lyotard, LeGuin notes the capacities for domination expressed in social dualisms that privilege one over another. She notes that Gethenian society has overcome the dualities that characterize state capitalist societies:

> Consider: There is no division of humanity into strong and weak halves, protective/protected, dominant/submissive, owner/chattel, active/passive. In fact the whole tendency to dualism that pervades human thinking may be found to be lessened, or changed, on Winter. (ibid., 93–94)

Overcoming hierarchical dualisms represents a step in overcoming hierarchy itself.

LeGuin notes that language itself can constrain thought, action, and choice. The Ekumenical investigator expresses this frustration that the "very use of the pronoun [he] in my thoughts leads me continually to forget that the Karhider I am with is not a man, but a manwoman" (LeGuin 1969, 94). Gender roles are embedded in language and this linguistic conditioning, too, must be overcome.

The androgynes, in LeGuin's conceptualization, free from sexual and gender constraint, rigidity, and conformism, have contributed "to produce a world without war, without rape, and without technological exploitation" (Parker Rhodes 1983, 114). This world is possible because the androgyne is essentially anarchistic in character. As LeGuin suggests in "Is Gender Necessary?":

> It values order without constraint, rule by custom not by force. It has been the male who enforces and breaks laws. On Gethen, these two principles are in balance: the decentralizing against the centralizing, the flexible against the rigid, the circular against the linear. (LeGuin 1969, 165)

This is an assertion of productive engagement, of lively balance or mutuality, rather than an either/or opposition.

The outsider Genly Ai eventually grows to appreciate, accept, even love, the androgyne. He becomes capable of seeing past attempts to impose a sexualized or gendered identity in the androgyne, seeing Gethenians thus: "not a man's face and not a woman's, a human face, these were a relief to me, familiar, right" (LeGuin 1969, 279). Through struggle Genly Ai is able to overcome the constraints of imposed gender.

All of this reflects an anarchist emphasis on process, on becoming, on possibility and potentiality ever in the making. It speaks against caricatures that pose anarchism as holding to a fixed notion of human nature as perfect. This is not about notions of perfectibility either, since, for anarchists, there is no moment of human perfection—no perfect human nature to be achieved and no perfect social arrangement free of power or decision in which matters are settled once and for all. Anarchists are not utopian. Thus, for anarchists, free and non-coercive relations are essential to ensure that opportunities for improvement and greater liberty are not foreclosed upon.

A key theme of *The Left Hand of Darkness* is friendship, particularly as expressed in voluntary political relations or what anarchists call affinity. According to Tower Sargent:

> The real basis for a decent society is such friendship, and in this sense *The Left Hand of Darkness* does at least imply that if one is to have a eutopia, it must be an anarchist one. (1983, 15).

All forms of government on Gethen are viewed negatively. This holds for the communist style government of Orgoreyn as for the constitutional monarchy of Karhide. The beneficial features of society are found in friendship and customary relations. Despite government practices, the people establish capacities for friendship and care. They also come to develop respect for the Other. Particularly, LeGuin examines the struggle for friendship between aliens as a human is introduced to Gethen. Friendship, though difficult, can be achieved and is, anyway, more important than laws and governments (ibid.).

Sexual essentialism becomes an impediment to understanding, care, and friendship. Sexual role definitions and the imposition of sexual identities impede liberation and restrict possibilities for a new society (ibid.).

The role of the anarchist artist

LeGuin has also been careful in her views of the role of literature in social change. She herself suggests that she never looked for specific, definable results in anything that she wrote (quoted in Killjoy 2009, 9). In reflecting upon issues of social prescription in literature, she has expressed caution regarding the potential use of literature as a model for social change, as some social realists have proposed. For LeGuin, literature has more appropriate and effective uses:

> My utopias are not blueprints. In fact, I distrust utopias that pretend to be blueprints. Fiction is not a good medium for preaching or planning. It is really good, though, for what we used to call consciousness-raising. (ibid., 10)

LeGuin does not worry about any pressures from activists to write explicitly radical political works (ibid.). Reflecting on socialist realism and art in the service of activism, LeGuin suggests: "Of course, I have been scolded by Marxists for not being Marxist, but they scold everybody for not being Marxist (ibid.).

In relation to questions of anarchist literature and her own activism, LeGuin is honest about her own limitations and strengths. As she recounts: "And activist anarchists always hope I might be an activist, but I think they realize that I would be a lousy one, and let me go back to writing what I write" (ibid.). This is a far cry from the pressures historically felt by socialists to create so-called "productive" socialist or proletarian art geared toward the perceived needs of movements.

LeGuin is convinced that artists cannot effectively use their talents in the pursuit of freedom within the context of hierarchical movements. Neither should they take their direction from would-be or erstwhile leaders. As she states:

> I think the pursuit of liberty is what the Left is mostly about. But also, I think if you really want to pursue liberty, as an artist, you cannot join a movement that has rules and is organized. Regarded in that light, feminism was fine — we mostly realized we could all be feminist in our own way. The peace movements, very loose and ad hoc, have been fine. (ibid., 10–11)

Le Guin explicitly rejects notions of art in the service of political groups. She certainly opposes any notion of art in the service of party building. Art is not art of "the Party." In her view: "I can't put my work directly in their service, expressing their goals. It has to follow its own course towards freedom" (ibid., 11). Like many anarchistic writers, LeGuin presents radical ideas in ways that avoid didacticisms or propaganda. Fiction can speak to the heart in a way that even the most realist non-fiction rarely does. Political writing requires a human touch that is often missing from leftist texts.

This is not to say that LeGuin's writing was naïve or avoided open engagement with political theories, or that she avoided political texts while working on a novel or story. In writing *The Dispossessed* LeGuin spent years reading anarchist texts. Anarchism explicitly informed her work and she actively drew upon anarchist political theory. As she suggests:

> I felt totally at home with (pacifist, not violent) anarchism, just as I always had with Taoism (they are related, at least by affinity). It is the only mode of political thinking that I do feel at home with. It also links up more and more interestingly, these days, with behavioral biology and animal psychology (as Kropotkin knew it would). (ibid., 13)

For LeGuin, her work can help to show the hypocrisy of political practice in liberal democracies. It can shine a light on the gap between the rhetoric of state capitalist hegemony and the reality of life under state capitalism. A Tower Sargent suggests: "We preach freedom and equality and practice coercion, hierarchy, and patriarchy" (1983, 33). Anarchist utopias can signal better ways of doing things, even where the alternatives are less than perfect and will require some work to achieve.

Chapter Eight

Staging anarchy

Anarchism and drama

Anarchists have used drama to express opposition to values and relations characterizing advanced capitalist societies while also expressing key aspects of the alternative values and institutions proposed within anarchism. Among favored themes are anarchist critiques of corporatization, prisons and patriarchal relations as well as explorations of developing anarchist positions on polysexuality, non-monogamy and mutual aid.

A key component of anarchist perspectives is the belief that means and ends must correspond. Thus in anarchist drama as in anarchist politics, a radical approach to form is as important as content. Anarchist theatre joins other critical approaches to theatre in attempting to break down divisions between audience and artist, encouraging all to become active participants in the creative process. Anarchist gatherings, conferences and bookfairs regularly include workshops on DIY theatre. Typically performances, often impromptu, are put on in the neighborhoods (often literally in the streets) in which such gatherings are held.

At first glance it might seem odd to associate anarchism and drama, especially given the negative media portrayal of contemporary anarchists as street fighting vandals in response to "black bloc" actions at anti-globalization demonstrations. Lost in sensationalist accounts, however, are the creative and constructive practices undertaken daily by anarchist feminist activists seeking a world free from violence, oppression and exploitation. An examination of some of these constructive anarchist projects, in which drama is part of a holistic approach to everyday resistance, provides insights into real world attempts to develop peaceful and creative social relations in the here and now of everyday life. In this drama plays a rich part, as a brief look at ongoing anarchist histories will show.

Drama and anarchy in the work of Emma Goldman

Among the important influences on anarchist literary production was Emma Goldman, the most prominent American anarchist. "Red Emma," who was herself influenced by Nietzsche, contributed important reflections on the relationship of drama and anarchy. During time spent in Europe during the 1890s, Goldman became enthralled by modern playwrights including Ibsen, Strindberg, Shaw and Hauptmann. So influenced by modern theater, especially the works of Ibsen, was she that her pioneering biographer Richard Drinnon was led to suggest that her anarchism was as influenced by the works of Ibsen as by the political writings of Kropotkin. During the political repression of the "red scare" of the 1910s, Goldman avoided arrest by using the topic of drama to address revolutionary issues (Goldman 1972, 15). Indeed, so interested was Goldman in the political potential of theater as a means for spreading and encouraging revolutionary ideas that her article "The Drama: A Powerful Disseminator of Radical Thought" makes up the longest entry in her best known work *Anarchism and Other Essays*. In fact "The Drama" easily eclipses other, supposedly more political works, such as "Majorities versus Majorities," "The Traffic in Women," and "The Psychology of Political Violence," that stand as recognized anarchist classics.

Beyond merely its length, the character of the article reveals the great value Goldman found in theater as a possibly crucial aspect of "the tremendous spread of the modern, conscious social unrest" (Goldman 1969, 241). Indeed Goldman glimpses in the modern drama "the strongest and most far-reaching interpreter of our deep-felt dissatisfaction" (ibid., 242). For Goldman, drama allows for a greater appreciation of social unrest than can be gained from what she calls "propagandistic literature." More than this, however, the development of social unrest into a widespread and conscious movement necessarily gives rise to creative expressions, such as dramatic theater, "in the gradual transvaluation of existing values" (ibid., 242). Goldman defines modern drama as a powerful vessel of radical thought.

This is part of Goldman's overall perspective on the place of creative production in broader movements for social change. During periods of broad social unrest and popular mobilization, as in the 1910s, 1930s, and 1960s there is typically a flowering of artistic expression, and revolutions in politics are accompanied by and spurred by experimentation in creative work, art, poetry, and music. For Goldman, the great spread of modern social unrest cannot be properly appreciated merely from a reading of propaganda literature or political writings per se. Such works obscure the rich vitality, purpose, and inspiration of the social movements and people who participate in or support them. To properly grasp the meanings of social unrest one must engage with broader forms of human expression as in literature, art, and, above all, in Goldman's view, modern drama. For Goldman, modern drama provides nothing less than "the strongest and most far-reaching interpreter of our deep-felt dissatisfaction" (ibid., 241). According to Goldman creative expression strikes to the heart of social ills presenting social criticism in a manner that surpasses what even the best propagandistic works can achieve. In her words:

> What a tremendous factor for the awakening of conscious discontent are the simple canvasses of a Millet! The figures of his peasants — what terrific indictment against our social wrongs; wrongs that condemn the Man With the Hoe to hopeless drudgery, himself excluded from Nature's bounty. (ibid.)

She continues:

> The vision of a Meunier conceives the growing solidarity and defiance of labor in the group of miners carrying their maimed brother to safety. His genius thus powerfully portrays the interrelation of the seething unrest among those slaving in the bowels of the earth, and the spiritual revolt that seeks artistic expression. (ibid., 242)

For Goldman, modern literature has played an inestimably important part in "rebellious awakening" (ibid.). Among the authors whose works embody "the spirit of universal ferment and the longing for social change," she counts Turgenev, Dostoyevsky, Gorky, Tolstoy, Whitman, and Emerson (ibid.). Note that she does not say *socialist* literature or even *anarchist* literature (as socialist realists might) Nor does she restrict her list to explicitly anarchistic authors, or even anarchist friendly authors, though some would count Tolstoy, Whitman, and Emerson among their numbers.

In the political magazine she edited, *Mother Earth*, Goldman sought to provide a forum for more than social and political analysis and commentary or agitational works. Recognizing the limits of traditional political discourse, Goldman desired to infuse *Mother Earth* with an imaginative and creative cultural spirit. Under Goldman's inspiration, *Mother Earth* would become a place for engaged discussion of art and literature. It would also be a place for socially significant and challenging art to find expression. In this the magazine would go beyond the narrow preoccupations and concerns of strictly political articles that have marked most political agitationals. In addition, the Mother Earth Publishing Association published new works by emerging artists, including poems by Oscar Wilde and plays by Henrik Ibsen (Goldman 1972, 14). Goldman often quoted Wilde in articles such as "Anarchism: What it Really Stands For." Goldman's references to previous eras are often literary as in her discussion of changed norms compared to the eras of Romeo and Juliet and Gretchen.

Goldman considered George Bernard Shaw clever and despite great differences between herself and the proponent of the Fabian state, she engaged him positively in her writings. She references Shaw's *Mrs. Warren's Profession* in her commentary on the sex trade, "The Traffic in Women": "Why waste your life working for a few shillings a week in a scullery, eighteen hours a day" (ibid., 144). Exploitation of labor, capitalist extraction of surplus value, is the real cause of the trade in women. Capitalism drives women away from the scullery, into the sex trade.

In contemplating a turn to prostitution in order to raise funds for Berkman's attempt on Carnegie Steel manager Henry Clay Frick, Goldman recalled Dostoyevsky's *Crime and Punishment*. The character Sonya Marmeladov's daughter had become a prostitute in order to support her younger siblings and to aid her sick grandmother. As she recalls:

> I visioned Sonya as she lay on her cot, face to the wall, her shoulders twitching. I could almost feel the same way. Sensitive Sonya could sell her body; why not I? My cause was greater than hers. It was Sasha — his great deed — the people. (ibid., 242)

In discussing the anarchist critique of marriage and the oppressive character of the institution, Goldman again turns to literary and dramatic materials, including Pinero's *Mid-Channel*, Eugene Walter in *Paid in Full* and Robert Harrick in *Together*. One of the most forceful modern social critics of marriage, Goldman presents it as a failed institution. She uses literary as much as social works to develop her point. She invokes Dante's motto over Inferno: "Ye who enter here leave all hope behind" (Goldman 1969, 228). Throughout her analysis she calls up dramatic and literary portrayals of what she calls "the monotony, the sordidness, the inadequacy of marriage as a factor of harmony and understanding" (ibid., 229). More than social analysis, her literary works reveal the deep character of social issues for Goldman, and they do so in a way that profoundly connects with people in a manner that social criticism cannot.

Goldman respects Ibsen as "the hater of all social shams" (1972, 160). In discussing marriage, she gives much consideration to Ibsen, particularly *A Doll's House*. As Goldman suggests:

> Nora leaves her husband not—as the stupid critic would have
> it—because she is tired of her responsibilities or feels the need of
> women's rights, but because she has come to know that for eight years
> she had lived with a stranger and borne him children. (ibid.)

Thus the individual and personal concern melds with the social. The dramatist portrays this in a more nuanced and affective way than the political commentator.

Goldman finds a great example of a free mother in Ibsen's portrait of Mrs. Alving of *Ghosts*: "She was the ideal mother because she had outgrown marriage and all its horrors, because she had broken her chains, and set her spirit free to soar until it returned a personality, regenerated and strong" (1972, 167). She was, of course, not able to rescue her love, Oswald, but did manage to realize that the only condition of a beautiful life is love in freedom: "Those who like Mrs. Alving, have paid with blood and tears for their spiritual awakening, repudiate marriage as an imposition, a shallow, empty mockery" (ibid.). The powerful portrayal of this struggle speaks to the restrictive character of marriage and the possibilities of free and open love more potently than the most astute political tract or speech, and does so through empathy rather than exhortation.

For Goldman, the modern drama is more far-reaching than painting or literature in the rise of radical thought and the spread of new values. A study of the development of modern ideas shows the power of drama in driving home important social truths that are otherwise overlooked or ignored when presented in other forms (Goldman 1969, 242).

Anarchy and O'Neill

The intersection of anarchism and drama is shown significantly in the works of Eugene O'Neill. Indeed anarchism is the primary, overtly referenced ideological influence on O'Neill's perspective. While O'Neill initially showed some sympathy for social anarchist movements, and looked favorably upon the writings of prominent social anarchist Emma Goldman, his primary personal commitment was to philosophical anarchism, which remained the greatest ideological influence on his thinking. Perhaps the strongest direct influence on O'Neill's anarchist perspective was Benjamin R. Tucker, the editor of the important anarchist journal *Liberty*. Tucker was the first prominent American thinker to identify himself as an anarchist. He would become the central figure in the emergence and development of philosophical or individualist anarchism in the US, introducing the works of Pierre-Joseph Proudhon and Max Stirner, among others, to North American audiences. Tucker was himself influenced by Stirner, being the first to publish an English language version of Stirner's work. O'Neill was introduced to Tucker as an eighteen year old and spent much time at Tucker's Unique Book Shop in New York City.

The eclectic collection at Tucker's bookstore exposed O'Neill to experimental and provocative works of philosophy, politics and art that were not available anywhere else in the US. Many of the works had been translated and/or published by Tucker himself. Tucker was the first to publish in North America Max Stirner's individualist classic, *The Ego and Its Own*, a book that was quite influential on the development of O'Neill's political consciousness. Tucker published the important libertarian journals *Radical Review* and the highly influential *Liberty*, which became regarded as the best English language anarchist journal. Tucker was admired by writers including Bernard Shaw and Walt Whitman.

Tucker's anarchism, unlike that of anarchist communist contemporaries Goldman and Berkman, was based on gradual, non-violent, rather than revolutionary, social and cultural change. In place of force, Tucker advocated the liberation of the individual's creative capacities. Tucker looked to gradual enlightenment through alternative institutions, schools, cooperative banks and workers' associations, as practical means to enact change.

Social change, for Tucker, required personal transformation first and foremost, a perspective that O'Neill himself claimed as a great influence on his own outlook. At the same time, while rejecting force, which he termed domination, Tucker did assert the right of individuals and groups to defend themselves against aggression.

O'Neill was convinced to abandon socialism for anarchism by his friends Terry Carlin and Hutchins Hapgood. O'Neill studied at the Ferrer Center in New York City, an alternative school organized and frequented by numerous anarchists, in 1915. That year he also served an apprenticeship at the anarchist magazine *Revolt* published by Hippolyte Havel.

A friend of O'Neill's, Havel is portrayed as Hugo Kalmar in *The Iceman Cometh*, in what one commentator identifies as "a rather nasty caricature" (Porton 1999, 12). Kalmar (Havel) is given to jovial, inebriated rants, as in his "soapbox denunciations" ("Capitalist swine! Bourgeois stool pigeons! Have the slaves no right to sleep even?," O'Neill 1999, 11) which begin as wild declamations and wind down into sound and sudden sleep. He offers this view of the anarchist future: "Soon, leedle proletarians, ve vill have free picnic in the cool shade, ve vill eat hot dogs and trink free beer beneath the villow trees!" (ibid., 105).

O'Neill draws attention to Kalmar's concern with maintaining a fashionable and neat appearance, "even his flowing Windsor tie" (ibid., 4), and the actual poverty of his material existence as reflected in his "threadbare black clothes" and shirt "frayed at collar and cuffs" (ibid.). Havel's life displayed the duality that has often characterized anarchist existence. In Havel, the aesthetic dreams of a new world, reflected in the cafes and salons was juxtaposed with the reality of poverty and precarious work as a dishwasher and short order cook.

Born in 1869 in Burowski, Bohemia, and educated in Vienna, Hippolyte Havel was a prominent organizer, essayist, publisher and raconteur within the international anarchist movement. Now a largely forgotten figure, even among anarchist circles, Havel was, during his time, at the center of the artistic and political avant garde in Greenwich Village.

Among Havel's innovations was the development of creative spaces in which anarchist ideas could be presented and discussed, beyond the didactic form of political speeches. Influenced by the salons and cabarets he had experienced in Paris, Havel set about establishing such venues in New York, on an anarchist basis. Havel gave particular attention to nurturing performances of various types. Havel viewed such spaces as crucial to the creation of anarchist solidarity and community. Indeed this emphasis on the development of a sense of anarchist community distinguished him both from individualist anarchists, who stressed personal uniqueness, and anarchist communists who focused on class struggle.

For Havel, cafes, salons, dinner parties and theater were crucial for the development of solidarity among and between anarchists and artists. Havel viewed artists and anarchists as natural allies who challenged the bounds of conventional thought and action, a challenge necessary both for creative development as well as social change. He advocated the idea that art was revolutionary, not strictly on a realist basis, as would be the case for the socialist realists who would follow, but through experimentation and abstraction as well.

O'Neill also shared Nietzsche's disdain for state socialist politics, inasmuch as its collective forms expressed the resentment of the herd. Nietzsche disparaged the anarchists and socialists of his day who were motivated by a spirit of revenge or personal weakness and fear. Speaking with indignation at their lack of rights, such anarchists and socialists were, in his view, too lazy or fearful to see that a right is a power that must be exercised, their suffering rested in a failure to create new lives for themselves. Socialism stood as a new religion, a new slave morality, in Nietz-sche's phrase. As in the case of Christianity, Nietzsche opposed the self-limiting, self-sacrificing characteristics of socialism that marked it as a new religion.

These criticisms are themes that appear in O'Neill's writings and state-ments on socialism, and anarchist communism, and are also reflected in his portrayals of these political movements in works such as *The Iceman Cometh* and *The Hairy Ape*. The slave mentality or sense that the powerless are more virtuous and thus must wait for an imagined salvation is reflected starkly in the hopeless longing of the characters in Harry Hope's bar in *The Iceman Cometh*.

O'Neill was also inspired by Nietzsche's views on art and theater and influenced by Nietzsche's view of Greek tragedy as Apollo's harnessing of Dionysus, the emotional element in life and art. Greek tragedy stood as the epitome of the creative force directing the passions (Dionysus).

Contemporary drama and anarchy

Through the years anarchists have shared Goldman's enthusiasm for drama as well as her belief that theatre is an important part of anti-systemic movements. Perhaps the most famous, and long-standing, anar-chist theatre project is the Living Theatre which has been operating for almost sixty years. Founded in 1947 by Judith Malina and Julian Beck, the Living Theatre continues to produce and perform works that uses experi-ments in theatre to pursue themes centred around the interaction of politi-cal processes and forces of love and mutual aid. Addressing issues of authoritarianism, oppression and resistance in social and personal rela-tions, the Living Theatre remains focused

> on humanity's millennial dream of uniting these aspects of life in a cos-mically inspired fusion that transcends the quotidian contradictions that have fostered the alienation that separates most people from the realization of their highest potential.[1]

1   This quote comes from the Sixth Annual Montreal Anarchist Bookfair, May 21, 2005. During the bookfair the Living Theatre gave two performances and was celebrated for its contributions to anarchism and other social movements.

As an experimental political project the Living Theatre has directly confronted and contested these issues. Throughout the 1950s, in the climate of McCarthyism in the US, the Living Theatre's venues were repeatedly closed by authorities. As result the Living Theatre developed as a nomadic and collective effort pioneering new forms of nonfictional acting rooted in actors' physical commitment to using the theater as an agent for social change. Dedicated to reaching the broadest of possible audiences, and committed to taking theatre beyond segregated specialist spaces, the Living Theatre has performed at the gates of Pittsburgh steel mills, at prisons in Brazil, in the poorest sections of Palermo and in New York Schools.

Among more recently organized anarchist theater projects, the "Trumbull Theater Complex" or "Trumbullplex" in Detroit is one particularly interesting example. Located in the low-income "Cass Corridor" in downtown Detroit, the "Trumbullplex" houses a cooperative living space, temporary shelter, food kitchen and lending library. The former carriage-house has been converted into a live performance space. In addition to staging more traditional forms of theater the "Trumbullplex" hosts experimental performances as well as providing a space for touring anarchist and punk bands and for public lectures. Recently the "Trumbullplex" has expanded adding a building in another part of the city. Significantly the Trumbull members use theater as a way to make connections with the working class residents of the Cass Corridor, offering a space for shared creative activities as well as a venue for spreading anarchist ideas and practices beyond the anarchist "scene." The activists and artists of the "Trumbullplex" are literally "building the new society in the vacant lots of the old," to quote a popular anarchist saying.

As exhibited in the activities of the "Trumbullplex," anarchist theaters are liminal sites, spaces of transformation and passage. As such they are important sites of re-skilling, in which anarchists prepare themselves for the new forms of relationship necessary to break authoritarian and hierarchical structures. Participants also learn the diverse tasks and varied interpersonal skills necessary for collective work, play and living. This collective skill sharing serves to discourage the emergence of knowledge elites and to allow for the sharing of all tasks, even the least desirable, necessary for social maintenance.

In the face of capitalist alienation and mediation of creativity, one of the options left is "to begin *right now immediately*, live as if the battle were already won, as if *today* the artist were no longer a special kind of person, but each person a special sort of artist" (Bey 1994, 43). So, anarchists make insurrections now rather than wait for their desires to be revealed to them at some later date. For anarchists this immediacy contributes to a widening of the circle of pleasure and un-alienated work.

Opponents of anarchism typically respond to it by claiming that it rests upon a naive view of "human nature." The best response to such criticisms is simply to point to the diversity of anarchist views on the question of human nature. There is little commonality between Stirner's self-interested "egoist" and Peter Kropotkin's altruistic upholder of mutual aid. Indeed, the diversity of anarchist views regarding "the individual" and its relation to "the community" may be upheld as testimony to the creativity and respect for pluralism which have sustained anarchism against enormous odds. Anarchists simply stress the capacity of humans to change themselves and the conditions in which they find themselves. Social relations, freely entered, based upon tolerance, mutual aid, and sympathy are expected to discourage the emergence of disputes and aid resolution where they do occur. There are no guarantees for anarchists and the emphasis is always on potential.

Chapter Nine

DIY anarchy

One may find it richly suggestive of broader social potentialities to note that in an era of multinational media conglomerates and gargantuan publishing monopolies a number of younger people have turned towards artisanal forms of craft production in order to produce and distribute what are often very personal works. Of particular significance are the "do-it-yourself" (DIY) means of production and exchange being developed by anarchist creative workers, involving collective decision-making as well as collective labor in which participants are involved, to the extent that they desire to be, in all aspects of the process from conception through production to distribution, usually expressed within gift economies.

As cultural commentator Richard Barbrook remarks, for participants in a diversity of contemporary social networks, DIY activities offer an opportunity for coming together, a shared outlet for mutual expression and unalienated labor. Contemporary expressions of the term DIY in alternative or counter-cultural movements comes from punk rock scenes and particularly their visceral attack on the professionalization of rock music industries and the related distance between fans and rock "stars." This anti-hierarchical perspective and the cooperative practices that flow from it are inspired by a deep longing for self-determined activity that seeks to avoid reliance on the products of corporate culture. Most powerfully associated, of course, with music, punk scenes have given rise to a variety of cultural expressions including fashion, art, and writing. It is perhaps particularly interesting that, despite regular prognostications of its demise in the digital age, the bound book has become a favored product of such creative labor. Beginning with a discussion of the perspectives of, mostly, young anarchists this chapter explores the post-political politics inspired by the anarcho-punk ethos of "do-it-yourself" cultural production.

Seeking an alternative to the market valorization and production for profit embodied in corporate publishing enterprises, anarchist DIYers turn to self-valorizing production rooted in the needs, experiences, and desires of the specific communities in which they are involved. In opposition to a consumerist ethos that encourages consumption of ready-made items, anarcho-punks adopt a productivist ethos that attempts a reintegration of production and consumption in specific sites and practices. At the same time their practice articulates what might be termed a post-political politics. This politics is post-political in the sense that it rejects notions of politics based on representation, in general, particularly representation at the level of the state. It is, thus, anarchistic.

As part of an attempt to rethink social organizing in the present context I focus on overlooked or underappreciated themes, priorities, and forms of creativity that pose important challenges to conventional thinking about politics. The key principles of contemporary practices that I identify and examine in the following sections of this work involve self-valorization, or creative work outside and against capitalist valorization for the market, do-it-yourself politics, as developed in anarchist and punk movements, and collaborative "ownership" and the gift economy. Taken together, these aspects of movement practice express a poignant striving for autonomy and self-determination rather than a politics of representation.

DIY anarchist literature

For DIY anarchist writers, writing is part of a range of activities. Writing is rooted within a matrix of action—it contributes to and draws strength from, but does not dominate, other spheres of life. DIY anarchists try to refuse the split between writerly and other worlds. In the view of anarchist DIY writer Carissa van den Berk Clark:

> I think the ideal artist is somebody who deals with day-to-day events. And I think that a lot of times they're going to have a lot more genuine and interesting things to say when they're immersed in the world instead of cutting themselves off from it. And in order to really get yourself into those writer communities, you kinda have to cut yourself off from the world because you have to spend so much time on it. (Quoted in Killjoy 2009, 135)

DIY anarchists try to work collaboratively. They challenge the myth of the lonely writer toiling in obscurity, alone with their thoughts (ibid., 72). They do not write for themselves as much as for their friends, comrades, fellow organizers, and neighbors. On collaborative writing processes, DIY anarchist writer Professor Calamity relates that it can be a slow and challenging process but one that is richly rewarding. It also helps participants to move beyond the sense of ownership, over the product and the process of writing, which marks much of creative work. In this way it is a bit of anarchy in action, challenging notions of intellectual property and detached individualism that characterize artistic production within the capitalist commodity markets. Professor Calamity provides a detailed outline of how the process has worked in his experience:

> When I write fiction, we usually talk first about the ideas and characters. We verbally hash out the story and then huddle around the computer and take turns typing. Someone not from the group then usually reads it and does minor edits and then we get together and talk about it in some detail. The writing group may go back and re-write bits of it. Sometimes I will write whole chapters and then a group will meet to discuss it and offer major edits and changes. Someone else will rewrite the entire chapter and then it gets 'filtered' again. It's a consensus process and you have to have a pretty thick skin to go through it. You have to give up ownership and see it as a real collaboration. It's funny — in many ways the collaborative process can be as creative as the actual wordsmithing and writing. I hate editing, but in a group it's a less grating process. Others despise doing dialog and so on; we try to compliment [sic] each other. You have to be able to laugh to make it work, even when you're writing serious or tragic stuff. (ibid., 73–74)

Professor Calamity insists that he only writes through a collective process. At the same time, this can take a variety of forms depending on who he is writing with.

Carissa van den Berk Clark has self-published and distributed the novels *Yours For The Revolution* and *May it Come Quickly Like a Shaft Sundering in the Dark*. Her work draws upon punk scenes, squats, and freighthopping. Her stories portray aspects of anarchist DIY lifestyles with which she is intimately familiar. She examines feminism as part of anarchist movements and punk subcultures. *Yours For The Revolution* was released shortly after 9/11 and addressed many of the issues of that time in a direct and immediate way.

An active participant in a variety of social change movements, she draws upon her own experiences in her fiction. Her commitment to anarchist values is reflected in the content of her novels. It is also expressed in the DIY production of her novels and distribution through anarchist infoshops, bookfairs, and reading groups. For van den Berk Clark, rootedness in real struggles is an important part of her creative work. In her view, and in the view of many DIY anarchists, it is important for a writer to write about what they know rather than relying on secondary information. The danger is defaulting to stereotypes. This is a warning for socialist realists who approach working class struggles from the perspective of middle-class or privileged observers or, worse, leaders.

She agrees that fiction can be a powerful way of presenting anarchist ideas. There remains for her the concern that outsiders will mythologize the movement or, as has happened historically, demonize it. Anarchists need to be able to tell their own stories in their own way — thus the emphasis on DIY literary work. DIY production and distribution also serve to avoid the corporate censorship of mainstream publishers and distributors. DIY also makes the books less costly and more accessible. As van den Berk Clark notes:

> Since printing each one was cheaper, I could sell them for $5, which was something I'd wanted to do so that anyone could get it. Books are so expensive, and it winds up that people read less because it just costs so much more to get a book then [sic] get a movie. (ibid., 128)

The anarchist writer is concerned with distribution as well as production. This is part of expanding connection with others, inside and outside one's community.

Fiction also helps anarchists to clarify their own thoughts or work out visions of a decent society in ways that might connect with others, particularly non-anarchists. For Jimmy T. Hand:

> I like to think that for one thing, fiction is a good way to work through various scenarios without losing the reader's — or writer's — interest. I hate reading theory, and I know I'm not alone in that. But I love learning about the history of anarchism, or how it could be practiced in the future. Fiction is great for that. And not just real concrete stuff, like anarchy, but for metaphorically exploring so much of the human — or non-human — condition. (ibid., 83)

Fiction can move past the distortion of mainstream media as well as the didacticism of much political discourse. For van den Berk Clark:

> I really just wanted to show that we have the potential to be like the Haymarket anarchists and all the massive political coalitions that came about alongside of them and that, if we do, we can get hurt. The book tries to show how governments actually hamper democracy rather than promote it. (ibid., 126)

For van den Berk Clark, writing should not take away from or dominate the other activities in which anarchists are, and need to be, engaged. As she expresses it:

> The book that I'm working on, it will probably be indie published
> again, because I don't spend my time in the writer's world, where you
> have the connections to get a big publisher to publish it. I don't want to
> spend my time there. I'd rather spend my time in the trenches. That's
> much more interesting to me. I don't want to quit my day job. (ibid.,
> 134)

DIY anarchists are concerned that writing fiction does not draw away
already limited resources from other, perhaps more pressing, tasks. There
is a sense that writers recognize that their writing time is, in some ways,
subsidized by the movement organizers, workers, and activists — those
who staff infoshops, attend meetings or rallies, organize workplaces or
help feed people. At the same time there is recognition that literary work
can, in fact, be organizing itself.

While writing her novels, van den Berk Clark has been actively involved
in organizing political demonstrations and community mobilization. The
organizing has informed her writing, offering topics, subjects, and inspiration. At the same time, the writing has informed the organizing — remind-
ing her that political organizing is about communication and must deploy
effective communicative styles.

DIY anarchist Jimmy T. Hand is the author of the novellas *In the Hall of
the Mountain King* and *The Road to Either Or*. Speaking of the intersections
of anarchism and fiction, Hand offers one approach that brings together
action and art:

> First of all, just like punk rock: never put authors on pedestals. Most of
> us writers are pretty anti-social, and it's almost like writing and fiction
> are the only ways we can participate in the anarchist debate. Also, for
> me, it's like ... don't just be an author. It's not enough. In the gift-
> economy anarchist society I'd like to live in, it wouldn't really be
> enough to say, 'Well, I write books' or, 'Well, I tell stories at night in the
> dance hall.' So? Do you grow food? Organize recycling? Dig up con-
> crete? Fight against capitalism? (Quoted in Killjoy 2009, 82–83)

DIY anarchists strive to overcome the division of labor between head and
hand, between professional artist and audiences of art. They reject the role
of full-time artist who does not contribute more broadly to the everyday
upkeep of a community.

Anarchists are not content to write books that will only appeal to other
anarchists. They try to avoid the temptation of subcultural writing and art,
to break beyond the insularity and self-referentiality of most alternative
activist art. As van den Berk Clark notes:

> I wanted the books to not just be read by anarchists; I wanted it [sic] to
> be read by kids in seventh grade. It was a story that seventh graders, or

high school kids, could read and they could relate to and also discover
that there are different ways to look at the world. One that doesn't
involve trying to become powerful, getting stuff or showing off. (ibid.,
131–132)

Van den Berk Clark notes that contemporary anarchists have a unique vantage point in that many are poor or experience low socio-economic status,
yet they are often highly educated, many having much university experience. Many university educated anarchists come from working class backgrounds themselves and are the first in their family to attend university. For
many anarchists, literature provides a chance to escape conservative environments, particularly the environments of their youth, while also communicating with the people who occupy those environments.

Many anarchist writers had unsatisfying experiences within academic
contexts. In the words of the DIY anarchist writer Professor Calamity:

It wasn't about ego, capital-A art, exorcising personal demons, or any
of that jazz. It was just fun to see where we could take ideas and characters. In college I took some creative writing classes but hated it. I
hated the egos and the pretentiousness. I wanted to tell stories and
share ideas, not compete to see who was the most clever or well-read.
(ibid., 72)

DIY also helps people to overcome the intimidation or lack of confidence
that many working class or poor people feel when confronted with the
prospect of writing or creating art. This apprehension can be worsened
where one's creative work will be judged by a publisher or jury. It helps to
overcome the self doubt or sense that literature is something produced by
others who are "more talented" or better trained, not something they
themselves might be skilled to do. DIY stresses that the voices of non-pro-
fessionals are worth hearing — in this way adding new perspectives to the
broader public conversation. In van den Berk Clark's words:

So anyway, I guess I always strove to write stories that prove to all us
poor slobs, us regular folks, that this is our world and we don't need to
take any crap. Yes, this world is tough but there's something within us
all which can bring about positive change. (ibid., 132)

Van den Berk Clark suggests that, for anarchists, one of the things that fiction can do is to "change who is admired and who is not" (ibid.). For DIY
anarchists, there should be no elevation of the artists above others in the
community. As Jimmy T. Hand suggests:

It's like, lots of people play music. That's one thing that is awesome
about our scene: most people play music. So at night when our work is

done, we all play music together, or maybe we take turns, but there aren't stars. Storytelling should be the same way. (ibid., 83)

For van den Berk Clark, anarchist fiction expresses certain key themes. Notably, these themes reinforce a DIY approach to culture and politics:

The messages I've tried to communicate have been: one, we're all in this together; two, that governments, especially large governments, basically exist to protect the rich and powerful; three, we are the only ones who are able to change the conditions that oppress us; and four, that we are able to create our own types of social structures. (ibid., 131)

Literature provides a potent art form for anarchists to communicate their ideas in a way that is emotionally resonant, beyond what political discourse alone offers. When asked what he hopes to accomplish through the writing of fictional stories, Professor Calamity replies:

I hope to accomplish the liberation of my brothers and sisters and the utter destruction of authority. Failing that, I hope to tell a darn good story that isn't too tidy. (ibid., 75)

Reflecting on the supposed "purpose" of literature, or what might be "accomplished" by anarchist literature, Jimmy T. Hand notes:

Maybe someone, somewhere, has read my stories and thought differently about something, and that would be nice, but if they have, they haven't told me about it yet. And that's alright; it's not about my ego. I mean, creation should be just that: creation. You make something, you give it to the world, and maybe it comes back to you somehow and maybe it doesn't. (ibid., 82)

Connection—to one's community, to one's fellows—is important. DIY anarchists try to avoid the distance and separation of commercial art—art for consumption. Even if the anarchist is not producing "high art" (or even "good art" for that matter), the fact of direct connection between interlocutors is important. For Jimmy T. Hand: "But just like it's best to relax to music by your friends and comrades, it's best to read escapist work by people you feel are your peers" (ibid., 83). The hierarchy that separates readers from writers while privileging the latter over the former must be dismantled.

The punks make books

The era of electronic communications, the Internet, and the World Wide Web has given rise to ongoing speculation about the eventual demise of the book. Yet many young people who have grown up on varieties of electronic media have turned to do-it-yourself book publishing as a collective creative process. Far from being an artifact or cultural object, the book presents, for participants in a diversity of contemporary youth subcultures and affinity groups, a context for coming together, a shared opportunity for mutual expression and unalienated labor.

There is sometimes a tendency to reify books by detaching them from the larger social milieux of their production. Books are presented as finished products with little if any attention to the cultures from which they emerge and of which they are a part. Punk book producers maintain a focus on the cultural contexts of production, even where that context is only a corporate "culture" to be critiqued.

So why have punk DIYers turned to self-produced books? The answers are many but they include a desire for cultural autonomy along with a preference for decentralized, local and participatory forms of communication and concerns over questions of representation. For many it is simply a matter of principle to rescue books, and the experiences that can be expressed in books, from the increased commercialization of "youth culture" and the merger of communication and entertainment companies after the de-regulation of media industries initiated by Ronald Reagan. While punk DIY is often associated with more ephemeral publications such as zines (self-made magazines) or pamphlets, many punk DIYers have favored books as more durable and enduring forms. Some simply enjoy the process of producing a book as opposed to the relatively straightforward production of zines. Many would say there is simply something satisfying about holding a book that you have helped to produce.

While cultural theorist Walter Benjamin spoke of disenchantment in the "age of mechanical reproduction," DIY publishers offer self-made books as expressions of re-enchantment or authenticity. This authenticity is grounded at least in the sense that such works help to overcome the division between head and hand that reflects the division of labor in a society of mass-produced representation. As attempts to overcome alienation and address concerns with overly mediated activities, DIY books suggest a striving for what an earlier era might have called control over the means of production and what has now come to include control over the means of representation. Perhaps ironically this has been aided by the availability of inexpensive desktop publishing and other means of "mechanical reproduction" since the 1980s (though not all punks choose to use it).

More often than not the punk bookmakers carry out their work in collectively run community centers, or infoshops — the modern version of the craft cottage right in the heart of the inner city. I have helped to produce books consisting of contributions to an infoshop "thought box" in which visitors are asked what they think about having a punk hangout in their neighborhood. A visit to an infoshop, such as Wooden Shoe books in Philadelphia or Uprising in Toronto will generally reveal a variety of original self-made books as well as reprints of punk (and often anarchist) classics. Contemporary punk publishers make long out-of-print books available as a way to share ideas and preserve histories and traditions that would otherwise be consigned to the trash bin of mass culture. In this way they are heirs to the long-standing practice of anarchist self-publishing, and many view themselves as such.

Along with punk DIY book production often comes the collective production of alternative subjectivities. For many participants the content as well as the process of punk book production expresses a confrontation with the cultural codes of everyday life. While punk books come in a variety of styles and viewpoints, they tend to present a vision of a desired society which is participatory and democratic. In production, content and, often through distribution in gift economies, they advocate active production of culture rather than passive consumption of cultural (or even entertainment) commodities. Self-production of books provides an opportunity for producers to act against the proprietorship of information. Most punk DIY books are produced as anti-copyrights or as "copylefts" and sharing of material is encouraged. Indeed as a key part of punk gift economies, the book takes on an important place in experimenting with communities that are not organized around market principles of exchange value. They help to create a culture of self-valorization rather than giving creativity over to the logics of surplus value.

In this regard I should also point out, given my earlier comments about electronic communications, that punk book-makers have used computer technologies to expand the bounds of the book as well as the limitations of distribution systems. In keeping with the desire to make books as freely available as possible punk DIYers typically make their books available on-line as PDF documents free for downloading by anyone who wants a copy. This is a central feature of contemporary gift economies in DIY publishing.

Opportunities and obstacles: DIY anarchy and beyond

DIY anarchists are also critical of anarchist practices, particularly those that are repeated reactively without critical reflection or consideration on their effectiveness. They warn about the emergence of customary practices that are carried out merely or largely because they are familiar or comfortable. While many see the value of the flourishing anarchist bookfairs that have developed since 1999, they remain skeptical of such self-referential "scenes" and critical of the sameness that marks many of them over more than a decade of practice. For many DIY anarchists, the bookfairs simply lack imagination (literary or otherwise). Even worse, in some cases, they have become little more than sales events, or markets. For Professor Calamity the bookfairs risk becoming irrelevant:

> I go because I like the people and out of some warped sense of duty to support any anarchist project, but I just can't see paying for a table to sell goods about overthrowing capitalism. (Quoted in Killjoy 2009, 76)

They risk becoming rote and formulaic.

For DIY anarchists, much of the contradiction of anarchist political subcultures results from a lack of creativity and imagination among anarchists in their approaches to organizing. For Professor Calamity:

> Yeah, I know we're all hypocrites but I'm not sure we should be so unashamed about it. So much of our hypocrisy seems to be simply a reflection of our lack of creativity rather than the result of some deep-seated, inescapable paradox. (ibid.)

From a DIY anarchist perspective, there are many things that could be done to open up the literary imagination in creative production and distribution. For Professor Calamity:

> Everything is possible. We could have fictional potlatches. We could hide books in the children's sections of libraries. We could have around-the-clock readings by authors on soapboxes. The money we spend on renting a hall could be spent on renting a copy machine and

people could scam paper and just copy what they want. What about trade for books? What if people stenciled a favorite line or title across the city in exchange for the book they wanted? In fact, what if that was the only way you could get the book? (ibid., 77)

For DIY anarchists, the key thing remains social change and the place of literature as part of change. Literary work, like other forms of labor should be situated within networks of cooperation and gift economies. Professor Calamity suggests:

Most radical authors I know say they write not for money, but to create change. If that's true, then we should be trading our books for change … not pocket change. If you want my book, plant some tomatoes in the boulevard or burn an SUV. That would be of real value to me, not some bullshit royalty. I am sure there are a million other things that could be done to change how we relate to distributing books and writings. (ibid.)

At the same time it must be recognized that there is an economic pressure toward sameness, even, or particularly within radical subcultures. This influences and limits not only authors but readers alike. As Professor Calamity suggests:

Because of the lack of money in our scenes, the books are often too expensive to take a chance on buying something you wouldn't normally. This leads to an unconscious ghettoization of our reading, since we're only reading things we think we'll enjoy. We're just rereading the same authors, publishers, and whatnot. (ibid.)

The result is that anarchism can become insular and self-reinforcing rather than expansive and challenging. It can weaken the critical and vital aspects of anarchism and weaken the potential message of anarchy.

DIY anarchists are keenly aware of commitments they have to the people in their lives and movements. Reflecting on DIY publishing and the lure of mainstream publicity, Jimmy T. Hand suggests:

I can understand how authors want to make a living off of what they do; I'm tempted from time to time. But what kind of bastard would I be if I wrote my story, which is completely inseparable from the stories of my friends and my lover, and then sold it? (ibid., 80–81)

For Hand, fiction and social reality here converge: "Besides which, the scenarios I fantasize about don't involve mainstream publishing houses existing at all. So wouldn't a story about a fantastic real life be undermined by its own distribution method?" (ibid., 81).

Hand describes his vision of a world of anarchist literature that contributes to building an anarchist folklore while simultaneously moving

beyond the familiar subjects of anarchist culture. He provides a detailed
reflection on anarchist culture:

> I have this concept in my head of a world where storytellers, or bards
> or whatever, wander around and tell bedside stories and fireside sto-
> ries to people, and recreate a kind of folklore. I mean, I guess anarchist
> culture does it already, but it seems like it's always shoplifting stories
> or trainhopping stories, or occasionally, and these are more fun, war
> stories of our resistance. But then, most of *those* stories shouldn't be
> told, because if no one is caught for a crime, no one should admit to
> doing it. (ibid., 82)

This is a vision of the self-valorizing social relations that might contribute
to a new world. It is only partly glimpsed in the here and now of the present but it expresses the promise that other worlds are possible.

Conclusion

There have recently emerged a compelling diversity of experiments with
alternative forms of social and economic organization, as part of broader
social struggles against capitalist globalization. These experiments provide
alternatives to capitalist economic rationality, if only in embryonic or
prefigurative form. Shorthose (2000, 191) suggests that these "micro-
experiments," such as those discussed above, present "the potential for a
more convivial and sustainable future as well as empowering individuals to
maintain a greater sense of economic security and an expanded sphere of
autonomy away from the vagaries of the market." These experiments go
beyond the ephemeral and ethereal manifestations of protest politics to
begin the work of putting forward an alternative infrastructure, both for the
day-to-day necessities of sustaining movements in struggle as well as to
provide a space for developing social, economic and political relationships
that prefigure the sorts of relationships that people would like to see replace
those that characterize those of contemporary capitalism. The networks,
relations, and spaces of DIY activity can provide the building blocks of the
infrastructures of resistance that are necessary for any radical, let alone revolutionary, politics.

The movements against capitalist production, the affinity-based relations they have developed, and their emphasis on self-valorizing activities, suggest not only an opposition to global capital's economic rationality

and its statist supports, but also express a yearning for economic, social, and political alternatives to that rationality. In addition they articulate theoretical alternatives to the hegemonic representation and interpretation that accompany it.

DIY publishing, and media more broadly, immediately and relatively inexpensively produced, contribute to the creation of alternative spaces and relations from which to counter hostile or inaccurate mass media representations of the subculture, counter-culture, or community. The anarcho-punk writers, publishers, and book-makers are not asking for improved representation, in the manner of some producers of "alternative media," but are instead trying to tell their own stories. They seek to *present* themselves. DIY anarchist publishers assert control over the means of re/presentation while challenging the very real material constraints on participation in the media environment.

Finally it might be said that anarcho-punk writing, publishing, and book-making, as well as punk books, offer what an earlier generation of anarchists called "propaganda of the deed." In the physical work of putting their works together there is also a symbolic production, a production of alternative meanings about culture, work and community.

Chapter Ten

Autoethnography

Writing an anarchist sociology?

For anarchists, the literary imagination is not only expressed in, and expressive of, works of fiction or speculation. The literary imagination can also be powerfully expressed in and through social sciences. Indeed, for the anarchist, social science should be engaging, expressed in a way that speaks to and contributes to social struggles. It should be more than public. It should be active. This perspective stands against positivist approaches to social science which stress distance between social scientists and their "subjects" and a detached approach to research. Nowhere have these opposing views been more apparent than within sociology.

Recently there has been much hand-wringing among sociologists over the future of their craft. Concerns have been raised that sociology has abandoned the public realm, has foregone its social commitments. Academic sociology has been dominated by claims of value neutrality. It has largely abandoned action and motivation. It eschews eloquence. Sociology, like other social science *disciplines* has sold itself to priorities of policy and the job market. The humanist concerns that once held sociology's promise have been left to dwindling fields of literature and philosophy.

Paul Goodman notes that some recent analyses have claimed that literature has become irrelevant in modern societies. It has been replaced by philosophy and history, which have in turn been replaced by positivist social science. Literature remains only as entertainment or decoration (Goodman 1971, 228). It is something to be read at the beach or while on holidays. Rather than contributing to agitation, literature is about relaxation. Its significance has been reduced to standing on bestseller lists.

The potential loss is significant. History has emphasized what has been, but poetry speaks what should be (ibid., 229). Positivism is resituated. As Goodman notes:

> As in a dream, people recall that technology is a branch of moral phi-
> losophy, with the forgotten criteria of prudence, temperance, amenity,
> practicality for ordinary use; and they ask for a science that is ecologi-
> cal and modestly naturalistic rather than aggressively experimental.
> But one cannot *do* moral philosophy, ecology, and naturalism without
> literary language. (ibid., 231–232)

As Goodman recalls: "It was only a few years ago that C. P. Snow berated
literary men for their ignorance of positive science, and now it is only too
clear that there is an even greater need for positive scientists who are literary" (ibid., 232).

The philosophical anarchist poet Percy Shelley offers a starting point for
a challenge to positivist sociology. In his *Defense of Poetry* Shelley proposes
poetry as a crucial aspect of liberation:

> The great secret of morals is love, or a going out of our own nature and
> an identification of ourselves with the beautiful which exists in
> thought, action, or person … A man, to be greatly good, must imagine
> intensely and comprehensively … Poetry enlarges the circumference of
> the imagination by replenishing it with thoughts of ever new delight,
> which have the power of attracting and assimilating to their own
> nature all other thoughts.

> We want the creative faculty to imagine that which we know: our cal-
> culations have outrun conception …The cultivation of those sciences
> which have enlarged the limits of the empire of man over the external
> world has, for want of the poetical faculty, proportionately circum-
> scribed those of the internal world … (Quoted in Goodman 1971,
> 229–230)

Literature might serve as a better guide for human conduct than the social
sciences, certainly more so than economics. As Goodman notes:

> But the broader function of literary language, including poetry, also
> remains indispensible, because we are never exempt from having to
> cope with the world existentially, morally, and philosophically; and
> there is always emerging novelty that calls for imagination and poetry
> (ibid., 231)

The global concern with technology and the positivist value neutrality
of the sciences (social as well as physical) in a context of global climate
change and nuclear proliferation raises the crucial demands that continue
to press upon the imagination. For Goodman:

> To try to cope with modern conditions by the methods of laboratory
> science, statistics and positivist logic has come to seem obsessional,

sometimes downright demented, as in the games strategies for nuclear warfare. (ibid., 231)

Goodman is harsh in his criticism of positivist sociology and the social sciences. As he argues:

At their worst, however—and it is a very frequent worst—specialist science and its value-neutral language are an avoidance of experience, a narrow limitation of the self, and an act of bad faith. It is obsessional, an idolatry of the System of Science rather than a service to the unknown God and therefore to mankind. Needless to say, such science can be easily bought by money and power. Its language is boring because what the men do is not worth the effort, when it is not actually base. Being busy-work and form-ridden, it has no style. (ibid., 233–234)

The recent developments of social sciences—driven over the last few decades by neo-liberal market imperatives and concerns of funding—are not the whole story. As Goodman notes:

The social sciences have been positivist only during my lifetime, though Comte talked it up a hundred and fifty years ago. Marx was still able to say that Balzac was the greatest of the sociologists. Comte himself was energized by a crazy utopian poetry. Sir Henry Moore, Frederic Maitland, Max Weber, and so forth were historians, humanists. Geddes, Dewey, and Veblen were practical philosophers. (ibid., 232)

There is much debate over the continuing contributions or relevance of modern sociology. For Goodman:

My hunch is that, despite a few more years guaranteed by big funding, it is moribund, done in by the social critics and the politically engaged of the past decades, who have had something useful to say. As one of the social critics, I can affirm that we are *philosophes*, men of letters. (ibid., 233)

Anarchists advocate deployment of the literary imagination within sociology as part of a return to engaged, rather than academic, sociology.

The social movements of the twenty-first century, as for the movements of the 1960s and 1970s, have made new demands on sociology as an active, engaged, humanist practice with responsibilities to social communities—including those too often marginalized by positivist science. Goodman finds chilling the appearance of great deeds with no meaning. He suggests: "What is exasperating is positivist clarity and precision that are irrelevant to the real irk. A value of literature is that it can inject confusion into positivistic clarity, bring the shadows into the foreground" (ibid., 236).

Among those things consigned to the shadows have been the experiences and meanings (and meaning-making practices) of the excluded, those who have been pushed to the margins within neo-liberal capitalism and the ideologies that sustain it. The neo-liberal "politics of exclusion," removes subaltern bodies from civil society and the realm of citizenship and public participation. Exclusion, being rendered invisible, immaterial, is a common experience for the poor and marginalized. Governments do not invite them to take part in discussions on issues that affect their lives. The comfortable chairs at "summits" on "living and working opportunities" are not filled by poor people. They are not asked to tell their own stories and do not get many opportunities to tell those stories. They are treated as objects rather than subjects. As Jean Swanson notes: "Poor people have as much control over government experiments or think-tank theorizing about their future as lab rats have in a cancer experiment" (Swanson 2001, 77–78). They do not ask which questions to address, they do not design the experiment and they are not invited to present the findings at academic conferences. As bell hooks notes, "we are afraid to have a dialogue about class even though the ever-widening gap between rich and poor has already set the stage for ongoing and sustained class warfare" (hooks 2000, vii). It is crucial that the silence be broken.

So we must present it ourselves. We must do autoethnography. Anarchists express autoethnography as a public sociology, as a means to relay stories of the excluded, stories that would otherwise be left unspoken. Oral traditions are strong among them and they can spin yarns all afternoon under the right circumstances.

Autoethnography: anarchism, sociology, and an emergent methodology

Postmodern research has questioned the privilege of dominant research methodologies for obtaining social knowledge. This has included a critique of traditional qualitative research practices. As part of these criticisms new research practices have been developed recently. Specifically, an emergent ethnographic practice, autoethnography, which involves personalized accounts of authors' experiences, has answered a call to give greater attention to the ways in which the ethnographer interacts with the culture being researched. Autoethnography is a form of research that connects the personal with the cultural, situating the researching subject within specific social contexts. Autoethnographers' texts, usually written in the first person, present their research as relational and institutional stories affected by history, culture and social structures (which are also affected by the researcher). The texts, which vary in their emphasis on self (auto), culture (ethnos) and process (graphy), offer means to closely examine self-other interactions.

Autoethnography finds its roots in the postmodern crisis of representation in anthropology (Spry 2001, 710). It poses a response to realist agendas in ethnography and sociology "which privilege the researcher over the subject, method over subject matter" (Denzin quoted in ibid.). As described by Ellis (1999) the work of the autoethnographer involves moving back and forth between a broad ethnographic lens focusing on the social and cultural aspects of experience and a more personal lens which exposes a researching self that moves by and through cultural interpretations which are often resisted.

By placing themselves clearly in the story, as agents from specific locations in processes of social and cultural production, autoethnographers have openly challenged accepted views about positivist "neutrality" and silent authorship. Indeed the "living body/subjective self of the researcher is recognized as a salient part of the research process, and sociohistorical implications of the researcher are reflected upon" (Spry 2001, 711). In autoethnography the researcher is firmly in the picture, in context, interacting with others.

Autoethnographies offer explanations of othering practices in research and an analysis of difference from "the inside." Autoethnography encourages a practical rethinking of terms such as validity, reliability and objectivity. Practitioners of autoethnography offer a critique of representation and legitimation within social science disciplines. These are perhaps some of the reasons that this emergent methodology remains controversial within social sciences such as sociology. I suggest that autoethnography offers critical researchers a useful new tool for understanding complex social relations in contemporary (perhaps postmodern) contexts.

While autoethnography has received growing attention within disciplines such as Anthropology, Literature and History, sociologists have been left on the sidelines of discussion around this emergent methodology. I view that as unfortunate since autoethnography offers a potentially useful methodological alternative as sociologists grapple with questions of community, identity, values and structure within the current context. It might also take sociological discussions of autobiography and biography beyond viewing these texts as resources or data towards discussing them as topics for investigation in their own right (Stanley 1993). The lack of comment from sociologists is particularly curious if one remembers C. Wright Mills' "insistence that unless sociology works at the level of biography it does not and cannot work at the level of structure" (Stanley 1993, 51).

In a work that predates most of the writing on autoethnography by several years, Stanley (1993) argues that sociological discussions of, what she terms auto/biography rather than autoethnography, have two parallel sites of origin. The first is the feminist concern with reflexivity within sociological research processes (as discussed above). The second is Merton's discussion of "sociological autobiography." Through his investigation of the dynamics of "sociological autobiography," Merton draws "analytic attention to the way that insider and outsider positions systematically influence what kind of knowledge is produced" (Stanley 1993, 42). These differently located and produced knowledges raise crucial issues for the sociology of knowledge, notably affirming that reality is not singular, it is not necessarily the same event for which people are only constructing different descriptions (ibid.). Stanley suggests that auto/biography "disrupts conventional taxonomies of life writing, disputing its divisions of self/other, public/private, and immediacy/memory" (ibid., 41). In her view, "'the auto/biographical I' signals the active inquiring presence of sociologists in constructing, rather than discovering, knowledge" (ibid., 41).

Crucial in this movement are processes of reflexivity, a key component of feminist praxis. Reflexivity treats the researching self as a subject for intellectual inquiry "and it encapsulates the socialised, non-unitary and changing self posited in feminist thought" (ibid., 44). In feminist praxis, conventional dichotomies or binaries which separate the social and the individual, the personal and the political, are refused. "'Personal life' and 'ideas' are both socialised in this standpoint, the conventional individualistic treatment of them being thoroughly rejected in favour of conceptualising them as socially-constructed and socially re/produced" (ibid.). Academic feminist work has focused on women's autobiographies in part because "feminism as a social movement is concerned with the re/making of lives, of inscribing them as gendered (and raced, and classed, with sexualities), and also with inscribing a wider range of possibilities for women's lives by providing contrasting exemplars" (ibid., 46). These have also been the concerns of critical sociological work.

Some of the sociological silence over autoethnographic practice might be the result of loudly negative responses that have been leveled by gatekeepers of sociological methodology. Perhaps the most vocal opponent in sociology, Herbert J. Gans asserts that autoethnography is "the product of a postmodern but asocial theory of knowledge that argues the impossibility of knowing anything beyond the self" (Gans 1999, 540). In light of the numerous examples cited above, this appears as a rather unfair caricature of autoethnography. What most autoethnographers argue, contrary to Gans, is the need for practices that actively and directly situate the researcher within social relations beyond the self, in which the self is engaged and developed and to which the self contributes. Instead of a self/other dichotomy, which Gans implicitly upholds, autoethnographers recognize the mutual constitution of self and other as relational concepts and seek to understand and express the processes by which they are composed and, significantly, might be recomposed or decomposed. What is presented is a reevaluation of the dialectics of self and culture (Spry 2001)

Gans also argues that autoethnography abdicates sociology's main "roles in, and for, helping people understand their society" (1999, 543). It is precisely this sort of patronizing approach, in which only (or mostly) sociologists understand society and the (other) people who live it must be helped, that has spurred some autoethnographic writing. Instead autoethnographers insist that members of marginalized communities have great insights into "their society" and the mechanisms by which marginalization is constituted and reproduced, including through academic elitism. Autoethnography seeks to situate the sociologists as the ones in need of understanding.

Instead, Gans (1999, 542–543) bemoans the loss of "researcher detachment" and "distancing" and contends that this leads to a loss of reliability, validity (and possibly funding). He then tries to disparage autoethnography by comparing it to social movements, as if they are negative aspects of society. Finally, Gans dismisses autoethnography as being "too ordinary to become part of any sociological canon" (ibid., 543) To that the autoethnographer might say: "Hear, hear."

While I agree with some of the cautions put forward by Gans, and indeed all methodologies should be approached with caution, overall his presentation of autoethnography is so distorted that it borders on caricature. Whether this rather one-sided reading suggests a specific agenda more than an open attempt at understanding is a matter for debate.

While Gans argues that autoethnography is inherently non-sociological, one gets a decidedly different perspective from Robert K. Merton's description of "sociological autobiography":

> The sociological autobiography utilizes sociological perspectives, ideas, concepts, findings, and analytical procedures to construct and interpret a narrative text that purports to tell one's own history within the larger history of one's times. (Merton 1988, 18)

He goes on to suggest that "autobiographers are the ultimate participants in a dual participant-observer role, having privileged access—in some cases, monopolistic access—to their own inner experience" (ibid., 43). Autoethnography has its sociological interest

> within the epistemological problematics concerning how we understand 'the self' and 'a life,' how we 'describe' ourselves and other people and events, how we justify the knowledge-claims we make in the name of the discipline, in particular through the processes of textual production. (Stanley 1993, 50)

Doane (2001) suggests that autoethnography juxtaposes memory and social theory, extending and embodying theoretical conflicts.

As well, Stanley (1993, 45) asserts that "focusing on 'the sociologist' and their intellectual practices and labour processes does *not* mean that we focus on one person and exclude all else" as Gans (1999) claims. Rather these practices and contexts can reveal much about the history of sociology, divisions within society, social networks and the social production of ideas (Stanley 1993). Autoethnography does not imply a shift of sociology towards individualism, contrary to Gans' depiction.

Autoethnographers suggest that sociologists situate themselves materially within a specific labor process and be accountable for the products of their intellectual labor. This also means acknowledging the situational and contextual production of knowledge and the sociologist's position within a social division of labor. The positionality of the sociologist is important for understanding each research activity. The autoethnographer is involved in the active construction of social reality and sociological knowledge rather than discovering it. For Merton, good sociological autobiography "is analytically concerned with relating its product to the epistemological conditions of its own production" (Stanley 1993, 43).

Autoethnography replaces the "power over" of scholarly authority, offering instead a "power with" the researching self and others. An autoethnographic text reflects a space in which "truth and reality are not fixed categories, where self-reflexive critique is sanctioned, and where heresy is viewed as liberatory" (Spry 2001, 721). It situates itself personally and politically. As one commentator argues: "It interrogates the realities it represents. It invokes the teller's story in the history that is told" (Trihn 1991, 188).

Spry offers an account of some of the benefits for research that she identifies with autoethnography:

> I am better able to engage the lived experience of myself with others. I am more comfortable in the often conflictual and unfamiliar spaces

one inhabits in ethnographic research. I am more comfortable with myself as other. (Spry 2001, 721)

While Gans (1999) argues that autoethnography will cause readers to lose interest in sociological texts, for autoethnographers a

self-reflexive critique upon one's positionality as researcher inspires readers to reflect critically upon their own life experience, their constructions of self, and their interactions with others within sociohistorical contexts. (Spry 2001, 711)

Still there are obstacles faced by practitioners of autoethnography in their attempts to develop alternative methodological practices. As Spry notes: "An autoethnographic voice can interrogate the politics that structure the personal, yet it must still struggle within the language that represents dominant politics" (2001, 722). In particular, "[s]peaking and embodying the politically transgressive through experimental linguistic forms (i.e. autoethnography, sociopoetics, performance scripts) can result in a lack of publications" (ibid.). Thus autoethnographers must often become advocates "for the multivocality of form and content in academic journals" (ibid., 723), against the academic preference for impersonal and nonemotional modes of representation (Goodall 1998, 6).

The defensive reactions of disciplinary gatekeepers, what some autoethnographers call a "backlash" (Rhinehart 1998), has had the effect of silencing larger sociological debate over the emergence and development of new methodological practices (Sparkes 2000; Spry 2001). It may also explain why some autoethnographies have been written recently on experiences with the gatekeepers of academic journals as authors have attempted to publish autoethnographic works. As Sparkes suggests, charges of individualism or subjectivism "function as regulatory charges against certain forms of sociology and act to reinscribe ethnographic orthodoxy" (2000, 30).

I would much rather see an open and honest engagement with autoethnography within sociology. Such an engagement would not shy away from critique but would at the same time address the challenges to sociological practice posed by autoethnography.

As Spry suggests, understanding human experience requires "a pluralism of discursive and interpretive methods that critically turn texts back upon themselves in the constant emancipation of meanings" (2001, 727). Researchers in disciplines such as Anthropology, History and Literature have turned to autoethnography as one means to address this. I would suggest not that sociologists benefit from this emerging method, but that we might also contribute to its critical development. Rather than reacting against the experimental and the personal in autoethnography, sociologists might do well to see this as a method suited to what Mills once called (unscientifically it seems now) the "sociological imagination." Clearly, we must question how sociologists can live up to Mills' crucial challenge to connect personal issues with public problems if we continue to disavow methodological practices that have no time for the personal experiences, concerns and contexts of the sociologist.

Post-structuralism on the margins

Notions of objectivity and neutrality don't have much meaning on the margins. Not when you hear how "objective" observers like social workers and psychologists talk about you or see (and feel) how "neutral" agents like police respond when a shopkeeper accuses you of causing a disturbance or loitering. The context of "objective" and neutral practices in a capitalist, racist, patriarchal, and heteronormative context is always apparent.

Nowhere in official accounts are the excluded portrayed as people with hopes, dreams, lives and loves who are willing to stand up for themselves: survivalists with a strong sense of self preservation and dignity. Nowhere in political, corporate or media accounts will you find that portrayal. It simply does not fit the essentialist depictions of poor people deployed in poor bashing discourses.

Life on the margins allows anarchists to see what is referred to as essentialism as allowing for the exercise of various forms of power, providing a unifying basis for various forms of authoritarianism. It appears directly in the capitalist notion that poor people are "essentially" lazy and must be coerced to work through mandatory workfare or retraining programs, or through the elimination of welfare programs and subsidized housing. They are essentialized as "thugs" and "criminals" and simultaneously as victims who suffer in silence. Even other modernist categories of gender, race and sexual preference are blurred as clothing, appearance and demeanor stamp people with an unavoidable class mark.

In response, anarchists do not adopt either the positive essentialism of Kropotkin (human nature as good) or the negative essentialism of Hobbes (human nature as bad). On the margins one sees both, often in quick succession. So-called "human nature," as it is lived is often in conflict with itself.

In one interesting approach Gayatri Spivak speaks of the notion of strategic essentialism. Being marginalized can make one practice strategic essentialism or, indeed, anti-essentialism. You know that what people, people with positions of authority and respect, are saying about you is inaccurate, ideological, wrong. Spivak advocates strategically speaking from the place of the subaltern, not too hard when you actually are one, while recognizing how this place is itself constructed by power.

Having the view of the subaltern because you are subaltern, encourages a poststructuralist sensibility. One comes to see, in experiential rather than theoretical, terms, the necessity of ending

> the kind of thinking that puts people into groups like, 'the poor,' or those 'on welfare,' or 'immigrants' or 'Third-World people,' or 'Indians' to justify treating them badly and/or blame them for poverty. (Swanson 2001, 8)

Post-structuralist critiques of essentialism open new possibilities for the assertion of agency and as such resonate with the experiences of oppressed and marginalized people, even if distances exist between them. They always have to fight off attempts to force fixed and false essences upon them. They have to fight to tell their own versions of things.

Conclusion

Despite its high sounding name, autoethnography is a street idiom. Almost every other street kid I know keeps some kind of journal. They record their lives, often as poems, sometimes as detailed comics and graphic novels that would put *Spawn* to shame. And they are not simply personal rants divorced from theory either. They seem to have an almost instinctive understanding of Bakunin, even if they have never read him.

Often the ideas that most excite are those that come from the anarchists. As one of my partners says, "When you live on the streets anarchism isn't an abstract theory, it's the story of our lives."

Suffering the almost constant abuses of authority figures, from police and social workers to shelter staff and psychologists, means that an anarchist, anti-authoritarian, perspective resonates very deeply with lived experiences. It does not share the distance of some Marxist approaches with their talk of political parties, vanguards and transitional programs (a phrase remarkably similar to the ones used by cops and social workers). It also lacks the distance and "neutrality" of positivist sociology.

Of course, some post-structuralists, most notably Todd May and Saul Newman, have outlined the family resemblance between post-structuralism and anarchism. Both anarchist and post-structuralist approaches emphasize the decentredness of power relations and an appreciation of the extensive character of power. They also share a critique of representational politics and a strong "do-it-yourself" practice that rejects deference to would-be experts. When you are on the margins you experience micro-power and you survive through micro-politics. Squats, graffiti, zines all sustain and help people continue the fight to survive.

Academic leftists or post-structuralists writing about class are often trapped within specialist jargon that prevents them from communicating with those of us whose perspectives are developed and expressed in experiential terms. Hopefully this brief chapter will help to bridge that gap, to open channels of communication, understanding, and solidarity. Part of these struggles over meaning involves recounting our stories, providing glimpses into the many "contact zones," streets, struggles and courts, in which our bodies live. Sometimes telling our stories, raising our voices enough to be heard beyond the streets still requires a good old fashioned bread riot.

References

Agamben, Giorgio. 2000. *Means Without End: Notes on Politics*. Minneapolis: University of Minnesota Press.

Alston, Ashanti. 2003. "Towards a Vibrant and Broad African-Based Anarchism." Available at: www.newformulation.org/3alston.htm (accessed September 21, 2006).

Antliff, Allan. 2001. *Anarchist Modernism: Art, Politics, and the First American Avant-Garde*. Chicago: University of Chicago Press.

Appiah, Kwame Anthony. 2000a. "An African Way with Words." In *The Poetry of Our World: An International Anthology of Contemporary Poetry*, ed. Jeffery Paine. New York: Harper Collins, 309–321.

—. 2000b. "Antonio Agostinho Neto (1922–1979)." In *The Poetry of Our World: An International Anthology of Contemporary Poetry*, ed. Jeffery Paine. New York: Harper Collins, 341–343.

Balogun, F. Odun. 1988. "Wole Soyinka and the Literary Aesthetic of African Socialism." *Black American Literature Forum* 22 (3): 503–30.

Barbrook, Richard. 1998. "The High-Tech Gift Economy." *First Monday* 3 (12). Available at: http://subsol.c3.hu/subsol_2/contributors3/barbrooktext2.html

Bey, Hakim. 1994. *Immediatism: Essays by Hakim Bey*. Edinburgh: AK Press.

Brown, R. 1985. *James Joyce and Sexuality*. Cambridge: Cambridge University Press.

Caraher, Brian G. 1999. "Cultural Politics and the Reading of 'Joyce': Cultural Semiotics, Socialism, Irish Autonomy, and 'Scritti Italiani.'" *James Joyce Quarterly* 171–214.

Chesterton, G. K. 2007. *The Man Who Was Thursday: A Nightmare*. London: Penguin.

Cixous, Helene. 1972. *The Exile of James Joyce*. New York: David Lewis.

Conrad, Joseph. 1967. *The Secret Agent*. Harmondsworth: Penguin.

Craig, David. 1975a. "Introduction." In *Marxists on Literature: An Anthology*, ed. David Craig. Harmondsworth: Penguin, 9–24.

—. 1975b. "Towards Laws of Literary Development." In *Marxists on Literature: An Anthology*, ed. David Craig. Harmondsworth: Penguin, 134–160.

Dietrik, Anne. 2000. "Wole Soyinka (1934–)." In *The Poetry of Our World: An International Anthology of Contemporary Poetry*, ed. Jeffery Paine. New York: Harper Collins, 367–368.

Doane, Randal. 2001. "Exhuming and Slaying Adorno." *Qualitative Inquiry* 7 (3): 274–278.

Ehrlich, Heyward. 1997. "Socialism, Gender, and Imagery in Dubliners." In *Gender in Joyce*, eds. Jolanta W. Wawrzycka and Marlena G. Corcoran. Gainesville: University of Florida Press, 82–100.

Ellis, C. 1999. "Heartful Autoethnography." *Qualitative Health Research* 9: 669–683.

Engels, Friedrich. 1975a. "Letter to Lassalle (18 May 1859)." In *Marxists on Literature: An Anthology*, ed. David Craig. Harmondsworth: Penguin, 210–213.

—. 1975b. "Letter to Minna Kautsky (26 November 1885). In *Marxists on Literature: An Anthology*, ed. David Craig. Harmondsworth: Penguin, 267–268.

—. 1975c. "Letter to Margaret Harkness (April 1888)." In *Marxists on Literature: An Anthology*, ed. David Craig. Harmondsworth: Penguin, 269–271

Fairhall, James. 1993. *James Joyce and the Question of History*. Cambridge: Cambridge University Press.

Feyerabend, Paul. 1975. "Against Method: Outline of an Anarchist Theory of Knowledge." Available at: www./pnarae.com/phil/main_phil/fey/against.htm (accessed September 9, 2006).

Gans, Herbert J. 1999. "Participant Observation in the Era of 'Ethnography.'" *Journal of Contemporary Ethnography* 28 (5): 540–548.

Gelvin, James L. 2008. "Al Qaeda and Anarchism: A Historian's Reply to Terrology." *Terrorism and Political Violence* 20 (4): 563–581.

—. 2010. "Nationalism, Anarchism, Reform: Political Islam from the Inside Out." *Middle East Policy* 17 (3): 118–133.

Ginzburg, Carlo. 1999. *The Judge and Historian*. London: Verso.

Goldman, Emma. 1969. *Anarchism and Other Essays*. New York: Dover.

—. 1972. *Red Emma Speaks: Selected Writings and Speeches by Emma Goldman*. New York: Vintage.

Goodall, H. L. 1998. *Notes for the Autoethnography and Autobiography Panel NCA*. Paper presented at the National Communication Association Convention, New York City, November.

Goodman, Paul. 1971. *Speaking and Language: Defence of Poetry*. New York: Vintage.

—. 1994. *Decentralizing Power: Paul Goodman's Social Criticism*. Montreal: Black Rose.

Hong, Nathaniel. 1992. "Constructing the Anarchist Beast in American Periodical Literature, 1880–1903." *Critical Studies in Mass Communication* 9, 110–130.

hooks, bell. 2000. *Where We Stand: Class Matters*. New York: Routledge.

Hunt, Geoffrey. 1985. "Two African Aesthetics: Wole Soyinka versus Amilcar Cabral."In *Marxism and African Literature*, ed. Georg Gugelberger. Trenton, NJ: Africa World Press.

Jahn, Janheinz. 1961. *Muntu: Outline of the New African Culture*. New York: Grove Press.

Joyce, James. 1966. *The Letters of James Joyce, Volume II*. New York: Viking.

Joyce, Stanislaus. 1958. *My Brother's Keeper*. London: Faber and Faber.

—. 1971. *The Complete London Diary of Stanislaus Joyce*. Ithaca: Cornell University Press.

Killjoy, Margaret. 2009. *Mythmakers and Lawbreakers: Anarchist Writers on Fiction*. San Francisco: AK Press.

Kornegger, Peggy. 1996. "Anarchism: The Feminist Connection." In *Reinventing Anarchy, Again*, ed. Howard J. Ehrlich. Edinburgh: AK Press, 156–168.

Kropotkin, Peter. 1910. "Anarchism." *Encyclopedia Britannica*, 11th edn. Cambridge: CUP, 914.

Landuyt, Ingeborg and Geert Lernout. 1995. "Joyce's Sources: *Les Grands Fleuves Historiques*." *Joyce Studies Annual* 6: 99–138.

LeGuin, Ursula K. 1969. *The Left Hand of Darkness*. New York: Ace.

—. 1974. *The Dispossessed: An Ambiguous Utopia*. New York: Harper and Row.

Lukács, Georg. 1975. "Franz Kafka or Thomas Mann." In *Marxists on Literature: An Anthology*, ed. David Craig. Harmondsworth: Penguin, 380–394.

MacCabe, Colin. 1979. *James Joyce and the Revolution of the Word*. London: Macmillan.

Manganiello, Dominic. 1980. *Joyce's Politics*. London: Routledge and Kegan Paul.

Mao Tse-tung. 1956. "Talks at the Yenan Forum on Art and Literature." *Selected Works of Mao Tse-tung*, IV. Bombay: Foreign Languages Publishing House.

Marshall, Peter. 1993. *Demanding the Impossible: A History of Anarchism*. London: Harper Perennial.

Martin, James J. 1970. *Men Against the State: The Expositors of Individualist Anarchism in America, 1827–1908*. Colorado Springs: Ralph Myles.

Marx, Karl. 1975. "Letter to Lassalle (19 April 1859)." In *Marxists on Literature: An Anthology*, ed. David Craig. Harmondsworth: Penguin.

May, Todd. 1994. *The Political Philosophy of Poststructural Anarchism*. Pennsylvania: Pennsylvania State University Press.

Merton, Robert. 1988. "Some Thoughts on the Concept of Sociological Autobiography." In *Sociological Lives*, ed. Martha White Riley. Newbury Park: Sage, 17–21.

Momigliano, A. 1993. *The Development of Greek Biography*. Cambridge: Harvard UP

Moore, Gerald. 1998. "Introduction." In *The Penguin Book of Modern African Poetry*, eds. Gerald Moore and Ulli Beier. Harmondsworth: Penguin, xxi–xxvi.

Mphahlele, Ezekiel. 1967. "Introduction." In *African Writing Today*, ed. Ezekiel Mphahlele. Harmondsworth: Penguin, 11–13.

Mutiso, Gideon-Cyrus Makau. 1974. *Socio-political Thought in African Literature: Weusi?* London: Macmillan.

Neuman, M. 1996. "Collecting Ourselves at the End of the Century." In *Composing Ethnography: Alternative Forms of Qualitative Writing*, eds. C. Ellis and A. Bochner. London: Alta Mira Press.

Newman, Saul. 2001. *From Bakunin to Lacan: Anti-authoritarianism and the Dislocation of Power*. Lanham: Lexington Books.

Ngara, Emmanuel. 1990. *Ideology and Form in African Poetry*. London: James Curry.

Nolan, Emer. 1995. *James Joyce and Nationalism*. London: Routledge.

Ojaide, Tanure. 1995. "New Trends in Modern African Poetry." *Research in African Literatures* 26 (1): 4–21.

Olafioye, Tayo. 1984. *Politics in African Poetry*. Martinez: Pacific Coast Africanist Association.

O'Neill, Eugene. 1999. *The Iceman Cometh*. New York: Vintage.

Osundare, Niyi. 1994. "Wole Soyinka and the Atunda Ideal." In *Wole Soyinka: An Appraisal*, ed. Adwale Maja-Pearce. Portsmouth: Heninemann.

Owomoyela, Oyekan. 1991. "Socialist Realism or African Realism? A Choice of Ancestors." *Research in African Literatures* 22 (2): 21–40.

Parker Rhodes, Jewell. 1983. "Ursula LeGuin's *The Left Hand of Darkness*: Androgyny and the Feminist Utopia." In *Women and Utopia: Critical Interpretations*, eds. Marleen Barr and Nicholas D. Smith. Lanham, MD.: University Press of America, 108–120.

Payne, Jeffery. 2000. "Of Knowledge and Pleasure Globalized: A World Tour of the Poetic Moment." In *The Poetry of Our World: An International Anthology of Contemporary Poetry*, ed. Jeffery Paine. New York: Harper Collins, ix–xxii.

Plekhanov, Georgei. 1975a. "On the Social Basis of Style." In *Marxists on Literature: An Anthology*, ed. David Craig. Harmondsworth: Penguin, 76–94.

—. 1975b. "On 'Art for Art's Sake.'" In *Marxists on Literature: An Anthology*, ed. David Craig. Harmondsworth: Penguin, 272–281

Porton, Richard. 1999. *Film and the Anarchist Imagination*. London:Verso.

Rhinehart, R. 1998. "Fictional Methods in Ethnography: Believability, Specks of Glass, and Chekhov." *Qualitative Inquiry* 4: 200–224.

Sallah, Tijan M. 1995. "The Eagle's Vision: The Poetry of Tanure Ojaide." *Research in African Literatures* 26 (1): 20–29.

Scholes, Robert. 1989. *Protocols of Reading*. New Haven: Yale University Press.

Serge, Victor. 1975. "The Writer's Conscience." In *Marxists on Literature: An Anthology*, ed. David Craig. Harmondsworth: Penguin, 435–444.

Shantz, Jeff. 2010a. *Constructive Anarchy: Building Infrastructures of Resistance*. Surrey: Ashgate.

—. ed. 2010b. *A Creative Passion: Anarchism and Culture*. Cambridge: Cambridge Scholars Publishing.

Sherry, Vincent B. 2004. *Joyce Ulysses: A Student Guide*. Cambridge: Cambridge University Press.

Shorthose, Jim. 2000. "Micro-Experiments in Alternatives." *Capital and Class* 24 (3): 191–208.

Soyinka, Wole. 1967. *Idanre and Other Poems*. London: Methuen.

—. 1972. *A Shuttle in the Crypt*. London: Rex Collings.

—. 1976. *Myth, Literature and the African World*. New York: Cambridge University Press.

—. 1988. *Mandela's Earth and Other Poems*. New York: Random House, 50.

Sparkes, Andrew, C. 2000. "Autoethnography and Narratives of Self: Reflections on Criteria in Action." *Sociology of Sport Journal* 17: 21–43.

Spry, Tami. 2001. "Performing Autoethnography: An Embodied Methodological Praxis."*Qualitative Inquiry* 7(6): 706–732.

Stanley, Liz. 1993. "On Auto/Biography in Sociology." *Sociology* 27 (1): 41–52.

Stratton, Florence. 1988. "Wole Soyinka: A Writer's Social Vision." *Black American Literature Forum* 22 (3): 531–553.

Swanson, Jean. 2001. *Poor Bashing: The Politics of Exclusion*. Toronto: Between the Lines.

Tower Sargent, Lyman. 1983. "A New Anarchism: Social and Political Ideas in Some Recent Feminist Eutopias." In *Women and Utopia: Critical Interpretations*, eds. Marleen Barr and Nicholas D. Smith. Lanham, MD.: University Press of America, 3–33.

Trinh, T. Minh-ha. 1991. *When the Moon Waxes Red. Representation, Gender and Cultural Politics*. London: Routledge.

Trotsky, Leon. 1975. "The Formalist School of Poetry and Marxism." In *Marxists on Literature: An Anthology*, ed. David Craig. Harmondsworth: Penguin, 363–379.

Walunywa, Joseph. 1997. *Post-Colonial African Theory and Practice: Wole Soyinka's Anarchism*. (Ph.D. Dissertation, Syracuse University).

Ward, Colin. 1966. "The Organization of Anarchy." In *Patterns of Anarchy*, eds. Leonard Krimerman and Lewis Perry. New York: Anchor, 349–351.

Weir, David. 1997. *Anarchy and Culture: The Aesthetic Politics of Modernism*. Amherst, MA: University of Massachusetts Press.

Woodcock, George. 1962. *Anarchism: A History of Libertarian Ideas and Movements*. New York: The World Publishing Company.

Index

ecology and control of own labor, 88
equality *vs.* commodification of, 91
fiction writing by, 87
Joyce's writing on, 73
liberation from gender roles, 92
marriage and free love, 101
patriarchal societies, 93
working class,
Conrad's contempt for, 27
consciousness, 38
culture, 14, 21, 28, 35
writing. *See also* autoethnography;
censorship
anarchist approaches to teaching, 50
children learning, literary
production, 51, 52

collaborative process, 108, 109
colloquial bravery within, 54
commodification and
discouragement of, 50
corporate and "Party," 51
finding one's own style, 55
reflexivity, 126
without essentializing, 43

Y

Yoruba, myths and traditions, 78–81, 84
Yours for the Revolution (van den Berk
Clark), 109

Z

zines, 18, 114, 132
Zola, Émile, 33, 56